The Hidden Teacher

Ideology and Children's Reading

PETER HOLLINDALE

THIMBLE PRESS

First published in *Signal Approaches to Children's Books*
The Critic and the Child (May 1991)
Ideology and the Children's Book (January 1988)
The Darkening of the Green (January 1990)

ISBN 978-0903355-55-1

The Hidden Teacher first published 2011 by
THE THIMBLE PRESS
Lockwood, Station Road, Woodchester
Stroud, Glos. GL5 5EQ U.K.
www.thimblepress.co.uk

Printed by Lightning Source

THE HIDDEN TEACHER
IDEOLOGY AND CHILDREN'S READING

Peter Hollindale is an eminent critic, teacher and essayist in the field of children's literature. His 'Ideology and the Children's Book' (1988), which received the Children's Literature Association Award as the outstanding critical article of its year, has become a standard reference for students. He has written a companion piece, and other new chapters, for *The Hidden Teacher*, which includes two associated articles originally published in the journal *Signal*. Among his other publications are critical studies of *A Midsummer Night's Dream* (Penguin) and *Henry IV Part Two* (Macmillan) and editions of *Peter Pan and Other Plays* and *Peter Pan in Kensington Gardens/Peter and Wendy* (Oxford University Press World's Classics).

BY THE SAME AUTHOR

Signs of Childness in Children's Books
(Thimble Press)

To

TOM

born 17 September 2008

with love, and hope

CONTENTS

Introduction

The argument of this book is that there is no such thing as a simple story, or a simple reader or watcher or listener. Every story we hear, by whatever means, is full of hidden signals, transmitted consciously or unconsciously by the storyteller, whether the teller is Jesus of Nazareth narrating a parable or a neighbour gossiping in the street. Stories are full of values, beliefs and attitudes, whether knowingly or not. And so are we as readers and listeners, even as young children, because we are constantly forming our own values, beliefs and attitudes from our own life experience, and our response to stories is affected and conditioned by them, whether or not we realize it.

Helping children to become alert and expert storytellers and listeners is very important, because it is part of helping them to take control of their own lives. Although this book is focused on stories published in print and on their readers, the ideas developed in it can be equally applied to other media. The arrival of the internet has suddenly made these storytelling and story reading skills more important than ever, because we have learned to our cost how vulnerable young people can be in what they believe, and what they reveal, in electronic interactions.

In various ways the following chapters try to uncover examples of overt and hidden signals in stories designed to be read by young people, and to illustrate how they can be better understood. In part they are written as contributions to an academic conversation between myself and other specialists in children's literature, and the three chapters previously published have been widely read in that way. But my intention is also to present ideas and arguments concisely and clearly enough to be useful to busy teachers and student teachers and perhaps some parents, whose important task it is to guide and train children and teenagers to become effective readers (and hence listeners and watchers) of all kinds of story. Now that children grow up to become public storytellers in their own right, to be a skilful 'reader' and 'writer' is more important than ever in understanding our world, and in the process opening up enhanced and lifelong pleasure and enjoyment.

The Critic and the Child

Of the making of many books, and of books about books, and of books about children's books, there is no end, and of the last two categories it can reasonably be asked, 'What useful purpose do they serve?' Utilitarianism is not always unintelligent and can be salutary. Where critiques of children's literature are concerned, it seems fair to ask that at some level they should further the purpose of enabling children to experience reading not as a weariness of the flesh but as (in every sense) a growing pleasure. Every year produces new studies of children's books, ranging from academic research and commentary designed for specialists to informal articles addressed to the 'general reader'. In this chapter the purposes of critical writing about children's books are examined through three collections, very different in nature, all published in a typical year. What are they up to, and how useful is it?

In his survey of contemporary criticism[1] Peter Hunt quotes Elaine Moss, who has, as he says, 'been very influential in her highly practical approach to reviewing, library work, and involvement with children and book selection'. In *Part of the Pattern* she wrote:

> I am . . . very happy to leave literary criticism to those who work in universities or polytechnics and who write for a committed and learned audience in respectable specialist journals. This is where real criticism belongs. That is where it is (dare I say this?) *useful*. (quoted in Hunt, page 190)

As children's literature increasingly becomes institutionalized as an academic subject, it is exposed to the same rift between marketplace reviewing and professional criticism that marks the public discussion

11

of adult literature, but two differences make the rift wider. One is the question of usefulness. Elaine Moss strongly implies that 'literary criticism' is useless to the practical business of enabling children to prosper as readers; if criticism is useful, by implication it is chiefly useful to other critics. While academics are free to pursue their own incestuous utilities, the reviewers, librarians, teachers and some parents are busy where it matters, with the kids.

Sadly, it would be hard to contest the practical everyday truth of this. But my purpose here is to urge every possible effort to link theory with practice. There will always be plenty of people with a vested interest in widening the rift, and I would like to see a clear commitment on the part of children's literature's professional mediators to keeping it as narrow as we can. At least we should try to be useful to each other, and therefore – directly or indirectly – to children. Since none of these three books purports to offer direct help with the successful encouragement of reading (though some of their individual items do), it seems fair to ask what assistance they can offer indirectly.

The second difference between marketplace and lecture room that marks off children's literature from adult literature is the question of formativeness. With rare exceptions, adults are not reformed, or re-formed, by the books they read, and significant re-formations are likely to be intellectual ones originating in nonfictional works where there are few subliminal effects to take account of. Although books form a relatively minor band of colour in the spectrum of experience for even the most avid child reader, their effects are necessarily more significant partly because the child has a more limited background of established prior experiences against which to set new ones, and is always in a physical, emotional and intellectual condition of *becoming* rather than *being*. Nor are considerations of formativeness removed if we artificially ignore the reader and focus on the texts. The books that children read are mainly about children, so that processes of formativeness are integral to the story as well as to its reception, and will inevitably figure in critical discussion. (This can be easily verified by looking at traditional critiques of novels about children that were patently not intended *for* children, such as *The Mill on the Floss* or *What Maisie Knew*.)

12

Readers like Elaine Moss who are working with the primary child audience are bound to be practically concerned with such developmental questions as the kind of emotional tolerance a particular book demands. But academic critics, using very different language for a very different readership, may be engaging with exactly the same important questions. They can have a field day with the eclectic and interdisciplinary nature of children's literature criticism, freely engaging with questions of psychology, sociology and political ideology, because the books are both *about* formative experiences and *are* formative experiences. Compared with adult literature, then, children's literature provides rich extra opportunities for intelligent developmental critiques but it also provides fertile ground for arcane theory and for populist prejudice. Both academic and practical approaches may be either very useful or worse than useless.

I shall try to approach the question of usefulness anecdotally. In her stimulating essay, 'Enigma Variations: What Feminist Theory Knows about Children's Literature' (*Signal* 54, reprinted in Hunt, pages 148-65), Lissa Paul observes, 'It's all very well to have an epiphany, but telling someone else about it is another matter entirely.' Suitably warned, I will risk the story of a personal epiphany.

One January afternoon many years ago I was window-gazing in the shopping streets of Cheltenham. It was my teacher-training year, and I was on teaching practice and ought to have been refereeing football matches or preparing lessons. In the window of an art shop I saw a picture of a boy, lying on his bed, reading. He was dressed in pyjama bottoms, spreadeagled over the bed in an attitude of rapt and intense involvement in his book. At the time I knew nothing about 'body language', but the artist had vividly caught the physicality of excited imaginative concentration. '*That*', I thought, 'is what I want to produce. If being an English teacher is about anything worthwhile, it's about producing *that*.'

It would be nice to report that I instantly entered the shop and spent my meagre student grant on the picture, which hangs over the mantelpiece to inspire my efforts to this day. Alas, life is not like that. I had a girlfriend in Oxford, a pub near the school that served good beer, and an invitation from the permanent school staff to join them on an outing to the Cheltenham Gold Cup. (It was a private school, and had regular half-holidays devoted to sport.) *Ars longa, vita brevis.* All the same, I have never forgotten it.

My epiphany in wintry Cheltenham was Margaret Meek's fault. The previous term, at Bristol University Department of Education, I had attended her classes and been introduced, for the first time as an adult and 'professional', to children's literature. We had read and discussed *Tom's Midnight Garden*, then a recently published book, and realized that something was going on that had not been going on when we had left school ourselves, three or four years earlier. It was the start of what has been famously (or notoriously) called 'the second golden age of children's literature', and at the very outset Margaret Meek was nurturing enthusiasm for all it offered to the reading child.

She is still at it. One of her later pieces, 'What Counts as Evidence in Theories of Children's Literature?', is reprinted in Hunt (pages 166-82) and is, among other things, a vigorous, insightful and unafraid updating of the challenges that face the children's literature critic. Another of Meek's essays, 'Why Response?', is the first chapter of the valuable collection *Reading and Response*, edited by Mike Hayhoe and Stephen Parker, and includes the following passage, which is germane to my purposes here:

> Critics teach us about reading and how they do it. At the same time, they privilege certain kinds of reading, the kinds that reflect 'the spirit of the age' . . . My point now is that pupils could, if we let them, show us how they learn the rules of the reading game; how they begin to take risks in trying out new generic forms, to tolerate uncertainty, to discover that texts have power, and to read against the grain of the writing in the spirit of the age, as we teach it.

Margaret Meek's writing and thinking have developed enormously since 1959, and – in no small measure because of her influence – the critical environment is unrecognizable compared with what it was. But already in those Bristol University classes there was the crucial connection, expanded with such energy and subtlety since then, between literature and the act of reading, which gave meaning and purpose to my own encounter with a picture.

If at this distance of time I deconstruct that meeting with a visual text, it seems in retrospect much more complicated than I once thought. In a brief review of its component parts I can find useful points of entry to a critical activity on behalf of children, and so to assessing the usefulness or otherwise of these three books about children's books.

First, it is clear that I differentiated the quality of childhood reading from that of adult life. My view then was, and intuitively still is, that of Graham Greene in his classic essay 'The Lost Childhood':

> ... in childhood all books are books of divination, telling us about the future, and like the fortune teller who sees a long journey in the cards or death by water they influence the future. I suppose that is why books excited us so much. What do we ever get nowadays from reading to equal the excitement and the revelation in those first fourteen years? Of course I should be interested to hear that a new novel by Mr E.M. Forster was going to appear this spring, but I could never compare that mild expectation of civilized pleasure with the missed heartbeat, the appalled glee I felt when I found on a library shelf a novel by Rider Haggard ... or Stanley Weyman which I had not read before. No, it is in those early years that I would look for the crisis, the moment when life took a new slant in its journey towards death.

One of Hunt's contributors quotes Robert Louis Stevenson, from 'A Gossip on Romance':

> In anything fit to be called by the name of reading, the process itself should be absorbing and voluptuous, we should gloat over a book, be rapt clean out of ourselves, and rise from the perusal, our mind filled with the busiest kaleidoscopic dance of images, incapable of sleep or of continuous thought ... It was for this pleasure that we read so closely and loved our books so dearly, in the bright, troubled period of boyhood. (quoted in Hunt, page 74)

The passages have similarities and differences. For Greene the intensity of absorption is exclusive to childhood; for Stevenson it is specially associated with childhood, but achievable by the adult also. For Greene the childhood reading pleasure is formative and influential; for Stevenson it is chiefly self-sufficient delight. As a student in Cheltenham I assumed a value in intensity of reading pleasure and was Stevensonian; nowadays I attach much more importance to Greene's sense of formativeness, and indeed of childhood epiphany through reading. Behind both these pieces, and forming a major part of my own response, was the assumption that if this experience does not occur in childhood it will never occur at all. In short, my 'reading' of the picture incorporated assumptions about qualitative differences between childhood and adult reading that we still need to know much more about.

I did not assume, I realize, that the boy in the painting was necessarily reading a 'book for children', though de facto he was by one definition reading a 'children's book'. Some of Greene's 'children's books' were romances for adults, and so were many of the books I read myself at twelve. I did, however, assume that the book in the painting was *fiction*. A plausible 'reading' of the picture (contradicted if at all only by evidence of body language) might have been that the boy was desperately mugging up French irregular verbs before school, while his mother was pestering him to wash and come for breakfast: but I inferred bedtime and story. Partly I did so because the picture was also memory: I had read in just that way myself. The subtext of my 'reading' (a natural one in the first weeks of teaching) was a moment of recognition that subjective experience had slipped away and been replaced by something professional and vicarious; the occasion included loss.

Finally, there was the fact that the child was a boy. If it had been a girl, the pleasure depicted would have been just as valuable but somehow less noteworthy: already, many years before the evidence of the Schools Council Report, *Children and Their Books*, I knew at first hand that girls were more habitual and committed readers.

I am arguing for the tolerance of complexity, which this recalled experience exemplifies. At the time I would have proclaimed the simplicities: that children's enjoyment of books was the object, and that practical reviews and well-stocked libraries and knowledgeable teachers were the way to it. I would have taken Elaine Moss's standpoint to extremes. But things were not so simple even then, as my deconstruction illustrates. Elaine Moss was herself a distinguished literary critic, and

16

Margaret Meek's classes were about books and adult reading as well as children, and I had read *Tom's Midnight Garden* as a novel, not only (and I emphatically do not mean 'not just') as a novel for children.

Over the years since then I have greatly complicated my own understanding of the reading process, and so has criticism at large. The complexities of modern criticism cannot be written off as a futile academic game. Some of them are, some not. There is good and bad Academe. People at the sharp end, where the children are, need ways of distinguishing between useful and useless complications, between those which advance understanding and hence effective work with children, and those which advance other things (such as political causes or their authors' careers).

Many of the essential 'notes towards acceptable critical practice' were presented with unrivalled lucidity and comprehensiveness by John Rowe Townsend in 'Standards of Criticism for Children's Literature', his 1971 May Hill Arbuthnot Honor Lecture, which is reprinted in Hunt (pages 57-70). This is a classic statement, very little of which has dated. In retrospect it can be read almost as the Inaugural Lecture for modern children's book criticism. Although, as Hunt observed in introducing it, 'radical shifts in critical thinking' have not surprisingly since overtaken it, many of these radical shifts are precisely those which have steered children's literature studies towards academic specialism, and therefore widened the gap between critic and child which Townsend's lecture bridged so admirably.

Townsend's statement is of lasting importance because he distinguished clearly between general critical competences (equally applicable to all critics of literature, for whatever readership) and those that place the children's literature critic in a special position. Writing about children's books demands a particular kind of self-awareness that is not required when writing about (say) Shakespeare. The nature of the task means that individuals are important, and easily tempted to transgress into undeclared personal involvements – of emotion, values, psychological history – which devalue their judgements. Ironically, some of the most admired works of academic criticism written after Townsend are seriously damaged by failures of honesty and self-awareness in these respects. Therefore Townsend's inaugural analysis is still an indispensable guideline:

17

Being only human [the critic] cannot possibly know all that it would be desirable for him to know; but he will have a wide knowledge of literature in general as well as of children and their literature, and probably a respectable acquaintance with cinema, theatre, television and current affairs. That is asking a lot of him, but not too much. The critic (this is the heart of the matter) counts more than the criteria.

In the light of what has happened to children's literature studies since Townsend wrote, I will try to augment his lastingly sensible statements of principle with an additional (and fearsome) code of self-interrogation for practising critics. No one could possibly satisfy all these demands. I certainly would not claim to do so myself. But I think we should all try.

When I sit down to write about children's literature and reading –

– Have I allowed space in my thinking for recovery of my own experience as a child reader? (The results need not be explicitly declared, but the presence or absence of the activity will announce itself anyway.)

– Conversely, have I avoided synthetic reoccupation of childhood, and monitored the 'childness' of my thinking?

– If I accept that children's literature studies are eclectic in their approach to current literary theory and reading research, have I ensured that my frame of reference is explicit and that eclecticism has not produced internal inconsistency?

– If I accept that children's literature studies are eclectic in their use of nonliterary disciplines, have I exercised extreme caution in deploying those in which I have no personal qualifications? Have I avoided using single named authorities to validate (or indeed dictate) my critical conclusions, and have I taken steps to verify that those authorities I cite are still considered reputable by experts in the field?

– Have I avoided treating hypotheses as if they were incontestable truths?

– Have I decided on, and made clear, the sense in which I am using the terms 'children's book' and 'children's literature' in a given context (accepting that numerous working definitions exist, and there is no single accepted one)?

– Have I decided on my understanding of the word 'child', given that the sociological and biological conditions of childhood are historically determined, inconstant, temporary, culturally diverse, and reversible? (Several essays in these collections proposed that children of the post-television age are very different from their predecessors, and even more radical changes have since followed the arrival of the internet.)

– When I refer to 'a book for children', which children am I thinking of? *All* children? (If so, could I argue an equal case that a book is for *all* adults?) If not, which age group, gender, class, race, nationality, first language, level of educational attainment, prior reading experience, do I have primarily in mind?

– Have I considered, therefore, the extended sense of the term 'implied reader' as 'implied child', and extended this in turn to 'implied childhood'?

– Have I maintained a distinction between relativist and absolute critical standards? (A novel for ten-year-olds is still a novel, and I should be able to hold both concepts in simultaneous play.)

– Given that much criticism incorporates confused generalities about the separateness or lack of it of childhood from adult life, have I avoided such generalities? It is likely that in practice I regard childhood as being in some respects different in *kind* from adult life, in some respects different in *degree* (most obviously of experience), and in some respects not significantly different at all. Have I used incautious generalities to mask necessary sub-distinctions to which in practice I subscribe?

– Am I bringing a personal ideology to bear? (Yes, I am.) Am I sufficiently aware of its influence? Have I made it clear enough to my reader? Have I where necessary argued it, and not merely assumed its rightness (even where the rightness seems to me self-evident)? On this and the next point, have I taken on board the connection between this principle of critical ethics and issues of didacticism, indoctrination and censorship?

– Am I bringing to bear the ideology of my time and place, my historical moment and location? (Yes, I am.) Have I tried to be aware of its influence?

– As a consequence of the last two points, which readings am I privileging?

– Is my valuation of children's reading linked explicitly with *storying*? Or does it include nonfiction and allow for the storying of verifiable documentary truth? Or is my valuation more closely related to *imaginative absorption*, regardless of whether its object is tales of mermaids or instructions for making a kite? Or is my valuation mainly linked to absorption in *verbal* process, and what value do I attach to pictures and illustrations? Is my valuation related or not to other, nonverbal, forms of language which children experience, such as pictures, film and music?

– Is my critical approach developmental (considering books as events on a continuum of learning and growth) or does it treat books as isolated single experiences? If developmental, which if any formal psychological schema does it refer to?

– What purpose do I hope this publication will serve?

Few critical undertakings could hope to pass such comprehensive tests unscathed, but they may serve to illuminate specific procedural inadequacies that seem important. Some of these questions – those relating to developmental processes, to the enlistment of nonliterary disciplines, and to the rash employment of hypotheses – elicit disturbing answers when we look at the example of *Children's Literature 18*.[2] *Children's Literature*, the annual volume produced in the United States by the Children's Literature Association, is in the advance guard of academic colonization of children's books. It follows stringently the formal guidelines for scholarly journals, and over many years it has published numerous excellent scholarly (and useful) articles but also a regular minority supply of sterile academicism. In children's literature criticism, it is an unmatched archive of the good, the bad and the ugly.

The main group of articles in Volume 18 shows this publication at its worst. With the shining exception of an excellent piece of bibliographical scholarship by R.D.S. Jack on 'The Manuscript of *Peter Pan*', the essays are chiefly devoted to psychoanalytical studies of children's books, and in one case an adult novel that happens to concern adolescence. Characteristically, the pieces refer deferentially and uncritically to particular authorities as if they represented unchallengeable truth, and as if the unfortunate children's author had become the hapless fictive mouthpiece for a chosen quasi-scientific reading of the psyche. Arlene Wilner interprets William Steig's 'Tales of Transformation and Magic' with confident reference to Piaget and Bettelheim with no allowance for the incongruity that many readers will perceive in the partnership. At the hands of Susan Petit, Tournier's *Pierrot, où les secrets de la nuit* is yet more disturbingly placed (admittedly as it deserves), being symmetrically amenable to a Freudian reading, a Jungian reading, and a heretically Christian reading, all of them dependent on the simplistic allure of trinities. Oedipal ingenuities are numerous. Richard Rotert's study of *Peter and Wendy*, which he calls *Peter Pan*, contains a representatively bizarre interpretation of the scene where Peter and Hook climb up for a mutual breather on Marooners' Rock: the ensuing duel 'complete[s] an oedipal scenario of castration'. There is much, much more.

After the essay section, under the heading 'Comments', the volume healthily argues with itself by presenting a set of short pieces that query the methodological basis of the whole enterprise. Some of the alternatives proposed, such as substituting Marx for Freud, are just as dubious as the psychoanalytic excursions in themselves, but one succinct and telling note of reservation comes in Michael Steig's 'Why Bettelheim? A Comment on the Use of Psychological Theories in Criticism'. This miniature essay should be circulated to all students following academic courses on children's literature, and I quote its most important observations. Michael Steig has just been discussing Arlene Wilner's essay, referred to above, and goes on:

> . . . we are distanced from the experience of reading when the critic fails to describe her own relation to either the theory or the interpretation.
>
> There is nothing new in the unquestioning acceptance and application of psychological precepts: literary critics have been doing it for years, whether the source of undisputed wisdom is Freud, Jung, Bettelheim or Lacan . . . The special problem with Bettelheim (also true of Freud to an extent) is that his supposedly scientific view of child development is fraught with values that can be called political and moralistic, a fixed set of ideas about how children *should* develop . . . this critic and all too many others keep the works they interpret at a distance by choosing to apply 'well-accepted' views of child development without considering that any theory of a universal pattern of development is open to serious doubts. (*Children's Literature 18*, pages 125-6)

An example of this suspect critical practice can be found in an essay by Steven V. Daniels entitled '*The Velveteen Rabbit*: A Kleinian Perspective'. *The Velveteen Rabbit, or How Toys Become Real* is a story by Margery Williams (Bianco), first published in 1922. In this story toys become real in two stages. The Rabbit's fellow toy, the Skin Horse, tells him about the first stage: 'When a child loves you for a long, long time, not just to play with, but REALLY loves you, then you become Real.' This duly happens to the Rabbit, who is really loved by the Boy who owns him. Loving the Boy in return, the Rabbit helps him to recover from scarlet fever. But once the Boy is well again, his doctor and nanny order the Rabbit to be burnt along with all the other infected toys and books. The Rabbit is rejected and despairing; 'Of what use was it to be loved and lose one's beauty and become Real if it all ended like this?' At this point the nursery Magic Fairy appears to take the Rabbit on the second step of becoming Real: 'I take care of all the playthings that the children have loved. When they are old and worn out and the children don't need them any more, then I come and . . . turn them into Real.' And with this magic the Rabbit becomes no longer a toy, but a rabbit indeed. Months later the Boy and the Rabbit see each other in the wood, the Boy half recognizing the wild rabbit as 'my old Bunny that was lost when I had scarlet fever!'

Margery Fisher speaks for many critics in being dismissive of this tale, finding its tone sometimes mawkish and observing tartly that the 'overt moral of the story has in the past commended it to many adults'. Daniels has his own reservations about it, and he bases his account of them on the story's failure to respond amenably to the psychoanalytical pattern which he imposes on it and which he derives from the post-Freudian work of Melanie Klein. One incident (or absence of incident) is crucial to Daniels' reading of the story. Just before the Boy falls ill with scarlet fever, he takes the Rabbit with him to the wood to play. While the Boy's attention is distracted, the Rabbit meets two wild rabbits and is overtaken by a longing to be like them, to see them again and jump about as they do. The incident is then left, and in the next section one paragraph describing the Rabbit's steady decline into love-mauled scruffiness is followed by the boy's malady.

This is an example of what Aidan Chambers, in his essay 'The Reader in the Book' (reprinted in Hunt, pages 91-114), describes as 'tell-tale gaps'. How the child might fill this gap is a matter for discussion. Daniels terms the gap 'narrational duplicity', and fills it with an unarticulated onset of guilt in the Rabbit because of his wishful disloyalty, causing a slide into the Kleinian 'depressive position'. The Rabbit's 'efforts at reparation' during the Boy's illness constitute a depressive response to guilt and a feeling of responsibility. The abandonment he suffers when the Boy recovers causes a shift to a Kleinian plight of 'persecutory anxiety', which may be more bearable than the depressive anxiety it replaces.

My account of Daniels' reading is necessarily compressed, but I hope I have indicated without unfairness the essay's systematic indebtedness to Klein, and its single-minded imprinting on the story of a Kleinian thesis, which determines both its meaning and its shortcomings. The authoritative psychological text, uncritically adopted, validates a systematic process of critical refashioning.

What is largely ignored in this account is the child reader, and the narrator's stance towards the child. A major clue to the essay's serious misreading (as I see it) lies in the assertion that 'it is for the most part from the perspective of the Rabbit that the narrative engages us in the story'. In her study *The Narrator's Voice* Barbara Wall sets out to reclaim children's literature for the child, and places value on the narrative voice that speaks to the child reader. The proposition is useful here. *The Velveteen Rabbit* seems to me a story consistently and successfully addressed *to* the child. And the child reader is placed in implied alliance not with the Rabbit (even though we are chiefly shown the Rabbit's perspective on events) but with the Boy: the true centre of interest is the child's perspective on the Rabbit's perspective on events!

In other words, the implied question at the very heart of the story is the child's: 'What happens to the toys I love when I realize with distressed compunction that I no longer need them? How do I cope with old love's loss of love? How do I grow out of something without hurting it?' To this almost universal episode of childhood anxiety the story gives an imaginative and consoling answer: it is the *Boy's* unspoken guilt, not the Rabbit's, that preoccupies the Narrator in speaking to the child. And if the moral is overt and finally reassuring, it is neither simple nor easy, being something like this:

> Love is a hurtful thing, but is wonderful precisely because it is hurtful. In one sense it lasts for ever. ('. . . once you are Real you can't become unreal again. It lasts for always.') But separations and endings are the hurtful prelude to independence and new growth – for the Boy *and* for the Rabbit.

In the 'tell-tale gap', miscalled 'narrational duplicity' by Daniels, the child has a chance to recognize in the Rabbit's impulse to independence and peer-group play an experience which replicates, explains and absolves his own.

At several levels, therefore, *The Velveteen Rabbit* is a sensitive and appropriate invitation to childhood self-forgiveness. It seems to me unsurprising that so many adults (misguidedly reading it as a story about the Rabbit) like or dislike it for reasons that exclude the child. Daniels' essay exemplifies both the danger of allowing a psychological reference-source to imprint itself on the reading, and the danger of omitting the pragmatic application of narrative theory and the presence of the child as narratee.

It is in fact the chosen 'academic' methodology rather than the formal academic procedures in themselves that makes this volume of *Children's Literature* unlikely to be useful in furthering the cause of child reading. However, one might reasonably hope for more directly practical help from *Travellers in Time*,[3] which is avowedly celebratory rather than academic in approach. This book is the outcome of the summer institute, on the theme of time in children's books, which was held at Cambridge by Children's Literature New England in 1989. Given that time was their theme, it also seems reasonable to expect some interest in narrative theory and technique, investigating questions of narrative time and real time. There are certainly numerous glimpses of what might have been, such as a perceptive and illuminating account of narrative structure in Katherine Paterson's *Jacob Have I Loved*. In practice, however, the bulk of the volume is occupied with loosely structured, self-indulgent musings by famous children's novelists about their working practices and authorial intentions.

Children's novelists, yet where, oh where are the children? One reads talk after talk, and the child audience is mentioned only in passing, if at all. This does not necessarily deprive the enterprise of value. Children's novels are indeed also novels, children's literature is literature, and can for many valid purposes be read in disconnection from its target readership. Exploration of an overriding theme is one such obvious occasion. But where then is the rationale for confining the event to children's writers (especially when some of them seek every pretext to mention 'adult' works)? Why, so to speak, adopt children as your badge of adult self-selection only to forget them?

The answer, it seems, is that the absent children provided a sense of community, and the ensuing 'critical' exercise is like community singing. The event quite obviously gave harmless pleasure and uplift to everyone there, and the atmosphere is one of half-declared childhood enthusiasms given a euphoric airing in the presence of the great and good. But disciplined criticism it is not, because the bonhomie and the living presence of so many authors wholly obscure discordant recognitions that some of the books discussed are very much better than others. Forum on behalf of children it is not, because children are barely mentioned. Celebration is what it is, a slightly defiant coming-of-age party for a literary form which is still not quite sure that the grown-ups have given it a doorkey, and needs to forget the children in order to prove how mature it is. For all the obvious pleasure that the institute gave its members, its proceedings still betray a lurking, treacherous self-doubt. I would say in all seriousness that this likeable, self-conscious volume reflects a persistent nervous desire for critical self-justification which retards the open, public cause of children and their reading.

Curiously and interestingly, the two really outstanding pieces in *Travellers in Time* come from contributors who are not predominantly concerned with children's literature, either as authors or as critics. If you seek the child's presence in this book, you find it best in the writing of David Lowenthal and Diana Paolitto. Lowenthal, a social historian and the author of *The Past is a Foreign Country*, establishes humanely and with fine intellectual clarity the connections that lay at the heart of the institute's concerns. Some of his formulations deserve classic status, above all this one:

> ... children must draw sustenance from their past, yet also put it behind them.
>
> They do so not just by confronting the present, but by constructing their own past and future. That mental process begins long before children can physically act on it. Here books are critical: they teach modes of travelling in time that encourage children to overcome subordination to adults and to the confines of familiar worlds. To read chronicles of others' times is not simply to escape for a while from our own time, but to embellish and magnify how we apprehend it. But passing time then renders childhood itself ever more foreign. We have to recover or reinvent the child within ourselves to keep the clockwork constraints of adult existence from taking over. (David Lowenthal, 'The past is a childlike country', *Travellers in Time*, page 81)

That is splendidly and usefully said. So is the work of Diana Paolitto ('the lone psychologist at this institute') on 'The Child's Perception of Time in Children's Books', which applies the work of Piaget (in particular *The Child's Conception of Time*) to the institute theme. This piece is a model of how psychology can be constructively used, not to regiment particular texts but to illuminate our understanding. Psychology is a rapidly changing and developing science, and in the future it is likely that Piaget, along with Freud and Jung, will be seen as a figure of purely historical interest. For the present, however, it does seem that Jung and particularly Freud excite the imagination of unwary literary critics and generate essays marked by credulous intellectual dependency. Freud now holds far more interest for literary critics than for clinical psychologists. By contrast, Piaget has the merit of being ideologically unexciting, and offers precise formulations which critics find helpful but not intoxicating, a guide to critical thought but not a determinant of it. Wherever in these books his influence has been intelligently accepted, the result is benign and illuminating, and brings real children from the shadows to the light.

In the course of this chapter I have referred in passing to several pieces in Peter Hunt's *Children's Literature*, a skilful blend of anthology and argument. This collection brings together some of the most outstanding individual essays on children's literature to be written since it first attracted any serious critical notice. The essays that are reproduced in full include academic pieces – in the very best sense of the term – as well as others with a more practical focus. Whatever their bias, they all without exception help our understanding of children's literature and its place and value in the lives of boys and girls. And if children's literature criticism is about anything worthwhile at all, it is about that.

1. Peter Hunt, editor, *Children's Literature. The Development of Criticism*, Routledge, 1990.
2. Margaret R. Higonnet and Barbara Rosen, editors, *Children's Literature* Volume 18, Annual of The Modern Language Association Division of Children's Literature and The Children's Literature Association, Yale University Press, 1990.
3. *Travellers in Time. Past, Present and To Come*, Children's Literature New England and Green Bay Publications, 1990.

Ideology and the Children's Book

IDEOLOGY.4. A systematic scheme of ideas, usu. relating to politics or society, or to the conduct of a class or group, and regarded as justifying actions, esp. one that is held implicitly or adopted as a whole and maintained regardless of the course of events.

– *Oxford English Dictionary*

I will start with an assortment of disconnected statements.

It is a good thing for children to read fiction.

Children's own tastes are important.

Some novels for children are better than others.

It is a good thing to help children to enjoy better books than they did before.

A good children's book is not necessarily more difficult or less enjoyable than a bad children's book.

Children are individuals, and have different tastes.

Children of different ages tend to like different sorts of books. Children of different ethnic and social backgrounds may differ in their tastes and needs.

Some books written for children are liked by adults.

Some books written for adults are liked by children.

Adults and children may like (or dislike) the same book for different reasons.

Children are influenced by what they read.

Adults are influenced by what they read.

A novel written for children may be a good novel even if children in general do not enjoy it.

A novel written for children may be a bad novel even if children in general do enjoy it.

Every story is potentially influential for all its readers.

A novel may be influential in ways that its author did not anticipate or intend.

All novels embody a set of values, whether intentionally or not.

A book may be well written yet embody values that in a particular society are widely deplored.

A book may be badly written yet embody values that in a particular society are widely approved.

A book may be undesirable for children because of the values it embodies.

The same book may mean different things to different children.

It is sensible to pay attention to children's judgement of books, whether or not most adults share them.

It is sensible to pay attention to adults' judgements of children's books, whether or not most children share them.

Some of these statements are clearly paired or linked, but they can be read separately in isolation. All of them seem to me to be truisms. It would surprise me if any serious commentator on children's reading were to quarrel seriously with any of them. He or she might wish to qualify them, to respond as to Dr F.R. Leavis's famous 'This is so, isn't it?' with his permitted answer, 'Yes, but . . .' Even so, I would expect a very wide consensus.

However, if this series of statements is brought to bear on the controversy between so-called book people and so-called child people, it will be found, I think, that most of them drift naturally towards either one side or the other. In particular, there is likely to be a somewhat one-sided emphasis on remarks about adult judgements and their importance (book people); about children's judgements and their importance (child people); about differences of literary merit (book people) and about the influence on readers of a book's social and political values (child people).

If these two little exercises do indeed produce the results I expect them to, much of the long-established division between literary and social priorities may come to seem exaggerated and sterile. We have differences of emphasis disguised as differences of principle. (This may have happened because the extremes of each alternative reflect a much larger public controversy about the chief purpose of education. People slip without realizing it from talking about children's books to talking about educational philosophy.) One result is particularly odd. By my own idiosyncratic but convinced reckoning, the statements which are left over, which seem not to bend towards the critical priorities of either side, are those which concern the individuality of children, and differences of taste or need between children and adults or between one child or group of children and another. It is a curious fact that these, the most obvious truisms of all, are also the most contentious statements. They are contentious because on the one hand they cast doubt on the supremacy of adult literary judgement, and on the other they suggest that we cannot generalize about children's interests.

It is very easy and tempting to simplify a debate until its nature becomes conveniently binary, and matters that are not associated by any kind of logical necessity, or even loosely connected, become coalesced in the same ideological system. Something of this sort has happened in the schism between child people and book people. In the evolution of debate, the child people have become associated not only with a prime concern with the child reader rather than the literary artefact but with the propagation through children's books of a 'progressive' ideology expressed through social values. The book people, on the other hand, have become linked with a broadly conservative and 'reactionary' ideological position. The result is a crude but damaging conjunction of attitudes on each side, not as it necessarily is but as it is perceived by the other. A concern for the literary quality of children's books as works of imagination has become linked in a caricatured manifesto with indifference to the child reader and with tolerance or approval of obsolete, or traditional, or 'reactionary' political values. A concern with the child reader has become linked with indifference to high standards of literary achievement and with populist ardour on behalf of the three political missions which are seen as most urgent in contemporary society: anti-racism, anti-sexism, and anti-classism.

If this is the general divide between book people and child people amongst the critics, a matching divide is said to exist between writers. The book people amongst authors – those who are said by hostile commentators to have produced the prize-winning, dust-collecting, adult-praised, child-neglected masterpieces of the illusory 'golden age'

– are those who write 'to please themselves', or 'for the child I once was', or, in C.S. Lewis's famous remark, 'because a children's story is the best art-form for something you have to say'. The child people amongst authors, on the other hand, would accept Robert Leeson's analogy between the modern author and the oral storyteller of days before the printed book:

> . . . is the public, the consumer, obliged to accept such a take-it-or-leave-it attitude, being grateful if the artistic arrows shot in the air find their target? What happened in the old story-telling days? If the audience did not appreciate the genius of the storyteller, did that individual stalk off, supperless, into the night? Actual experience of story-telling suggests something different. You match story to audience, as far as you can.

The trouble with this packaging of attitudes is that it oversimplifies, trivializes and restricts the boundaries of debate. Admittedly most writers on both sides of the notional divide have at times unwisely offered hostages to fortune. One may take for instance Fred Inglis's remark:

> Irrespective of what the child makes of an experience, the adult wants to judge it for himself, and so doing means judging it for itself. This judgement comes first, and it is at least logically separable from doing the reckoning for children. *Tom's Midnight Garden* and *Puck of Pook's Hill* are wonderful books, whether or not your child can make head or tail of them.

This carefully formulated and entirely sensible statement offers an important distinction between equally valid but separate ways of reviewing literary experience. Yet I have seen the last sentence removed from its context and made to seem like a wanton dismissal of the child, a typical instance of the book person's negligent aesthetics.

On the other side of the chasm is Bob Dixon, who follows an assault on ancient symbolic and metaphorical uses of the word 'black' by a paragraph that seems ready on ideological grounds to consign Shakespeare and Dickens to the incinerator:

Adult literature, as might be expected, is full of such figurative and symbolic usages – when it isn't openly racist. Shylock and Fagin, Othello and Caliban all deserve a second look, for there's no need for anyone to accept racism in literature, not even if expressed in deathless blank verse.

This is quite true. Any individual is free to elevate political judgement above literary judgement, and to be contemptuous of all literature that offends a political criterion. The converse is also true. Any individual is free to like and admire a great work of literature, even if its ideology is repellent. These are the private freedoms of a democratic society, and I hope that any commentator would defend both with equal enthusiasm. I make the second choice myself in the case of D.H. Lawrence, whom I admire as a great writer and whose ideology I detest. Neither principle is much use when we confront the problem of introducing children to great works of the past that do not entirely accord with current moral priorities. But if anyone says, 'We should not introduce them; we should ban them,' I begin to hear the boots of Nazis faintly treading, no matter what colour their uniforms.

My particular concern in this chapter is to argue that, in the very period when developments in literary theory have made us aware of the omnipresence of ideology in all literature, and the impossibility of confining its occurrence to visible explicit features of a text, the study of ideology in children's literature has been increasingly restricted to such surface features by the polarities of critical debate. A desire on the part of the child people for a particular set of social outcomes has led to pressure for a literature to fit them, and a simplistic view of the manner in which a book's ideology is carried. In turn, this inevitably leads to a situation where too much stress is placed on *what* children read and too little on *how* they read it. At the very point in history when education seemed ready to accept the reading of fiction as a complex, important, but teachable skill, the extremities of critical opinion have devalued the element of skill in favour of the mere external substance.

Diversity and individuality

Things can be made to sound very easy, as they do in Robert Leeson's reassuring comments:

This is a special literature. Its writers have special status in home and school, free to influence without direct responsibility for upbringing and care. This should not engender irresponsibility – on the contrary. It is very much a matter of respect, on the one hand for the fears and concerns of those who bring up and educate children, and on the other for the creative freedom of those whose lives are spent writing for them. I have generally found in discussion with parents or teachers, including those critical of or hostile to my work, that these respects are mutual.

I should like to think that this was true and generally accepted. But it cannot, no matter how true, be so simple. In a socially and culturally, politically and racially fragmented country such as Britain (and most Western countries to some extent or other) there is not a uniform pattern of 'fears and concerns' on the part of 'those who bring up and educate children'. The 'fears and concerns' of a teacher in a preparatory school in Hampshire are likely to be substantially different from those of a primary school teacher in Liverpool; those of an Irish Catholic parent in Belfast will differ from those of an Asian parent in Bradford. I wish to make only the obvious but neglected point, that the same book, read by four children in the care of these four adults, will not in practice be the same book. It will be four different books. Each of these children needs and deserves a literature, but the literature that meets their needs is unlikely to be a homogeneous one.

It is of course important too for the writer's creative freedom to be respected. But in order to be respected it must be understood, and on that score also I do not share Robert Leeson's optimism. There is too much evidence of pressure on writers (from all points of the politico-moral spectrum) to conform to a predetermined ideology issuing in visible and openly apparent features of the text. Here, for example, is Nina Bawden, a writer widely admired by critics of very different approaches (see Fred Inglis, *The Promise of Happiness*, pages 267-70, and Robert Leeson, *Reading and Righting*, page 122):

Speaking to people who care, often deeply, for children, I have begun to feel that the *child* I write for is mysteriously absent . . . 'Are you concerned, when you write, to see that girls are not forced into feminine role-playing.' 'What about the sexuality of children?' 'All writers are middle class, at least by the time they have become successful as writers, so what use are their books to working class/deprived/emotionally or educationally backward children?' 'Writers should write about modern (*sic*) problems, like drugs, schoolgirl pregnancies. Aren't the books you write rather escapist?' 'What do you know about the problems of the child in the high-rise flat since you have not lived in one?' To take this last question. The reply, that you project your imagination, is seldom taken as adequate; but what other one is there?

Leeson's dictum, 'You match story to audience, as far as you can', is less straightforward than it seems. A diversity of authors exercising their 'creative freedom' – as they must, if they are to write anything worthwhile at all – will *only* match story to audience '*as far as they can*'. If there were indeed a single, uniform audience, a theoretical 'child' who stood for all children, there would be few problems. Either a writer would be able to match her story to this 'child', in which case her credentials as a children's writer would be proved, or she would not be able to, in which case she might have to settle for being a writer of those other children's books supposedly beloved of the book people, the ones admired by literary adults but unread by actual children.

However, one point I hoped to make with my opening anthology of truisms is that the most conspicuous truisms of all are ones many adult commentators are in practice loth to accept. When Leeson says 'you match story to audience', he must surely be postulating many possible audiences, whether individual (parent reading to child) or socially grouped (teacher or visiting author reading to school class). It is clear that these audiences will differ greatly from each other, whether in age, or sex, or race, or social class, and that these different audiences will perceive the same story in different ways. Otherwise there would be no need for Robert Leeson to do any 'matching'. He is not suggesting that a writer who adjusts and improvises in order to make his story work with one group of children can then sit back, assured of its success with every other group thereafter. And yet at their own self-caricaturing extremes this is precisely the assumption on which both book people and child people seem to act.

For the caricatured book person (a *rara avis*, perhaps) the distinguished children's book has a quality of verbal imagination which can be shown to exist by adult interpretative analysis, and this is a transferable objective merit which the 'ideal' child reader (though unable of course to verbalize his experience) is capable of appreciating and enjoying. The good literary text has an external existence that transcends the difference between reader and reader, even between child and adult. Consequently there is an implicit definition of children's literature which has little *necessarily* to do with children: it is not the title of a readership but of a genre, collateral perhaps with fable or fantasy. Ideology will be admitted to have a place in it, but since the child audience and hence the teaching function are subordinate to literary and aesthetic considerations, it is a small part of the critic's responsibility to evaluate it.

For the caricatured child person the book exists chiefly in terms of audience response. The distinguished children's book is one which the 'kids' will like and which will aid their social growth. Historical periods will differ in the forms of social growth they cherish, but it is an article of faith that the current period will be wiser than its predecessors. The child audience, by some ideological sleight of hand, will be virtually identical or at the very least highly compatible with the preferred social objectives. In an age that desires to propagate imperialist sentiments, children will be an army of incipient colonizing pioneers. In an age that wishes to abolish differences between sexes, races and classes, the readership is a composite 'child' which is willing to be anti-sexist, anti-racist and anti-classist, and does not itself belong to any sex, or race, or class other than those which the equalizing literature is seeking to promote. The 'kids' are a Kid, who is sexless but female, colourless but black, classless but proletarian. Children's literature is implicitly defined as being for this Kid: it is not the title of a genre but of a readership. Ideology is all-important to it. Literary merit will be admitted to have a place, but it is a minor part of the critic's responsibility to evaluate it.

Both these caricatures exist. Both are extremely intolerant of anything outside their preferred agenda. The first kind says 'I am almost inclined to set it up as a canon that a children's story which is enjoyed only by children is a bad children's story.' The second kind says, as someone did of Robert Westall's brilliant antitotalitarian story *Futuretrack 5*, 'The book will appeal greatly to teenage boys, which is the best reason for not buying it.' Both (though naturally for very different reasons) will abominate Enid Blyton, and perhaps it is true to say that both understand the effective working of ideology less well than she did, in practice if not in theory.

My purpose here is emphatically not to argue for or against any single ideological structure in children's books (and certainly not to vindicate Miss Blyton's), but to contend that ideology is an inevitable, untameable and largely uncontrollable factor in the transaction between books and children, and that it is so because of the multiplicity and diversity of both 'book' and 'child' and of the social world in which each of these seductive abstractions takes a plenitude of individual forms. Our priority in the world of children's books should not be to promote ideology but to understand it, and find ways of helping others to understand it, including the children themselves.

Three levels of ideology

Ideology, then, is present in a children's book in three main ways. The first and most tractable is made up of the explicit social, political or moral beliefs of the individual writer, and his wish to recommend them to children through the story. An attractive example is this, offered by the late Henry Treece:

> I feel that children will come to no harm if, in their stories, an ultimate justice is shown to prevail, if, in spite of hard times, the characters come through to receive what they deserve. This, after all, is a hope which most of us share – that all may yet be well provided that we press on with courage and faith. So in my stories I try to tell the children that life may be difficult and unpredictable, and that even the most commendable characters may suffer injustice and misery for a while, but that the joy is in the doing, the effort, and that self-pity has no place. And at the

end and the gods willing, the good man who holds to the permanent virtues of truthfulness, loyalty and a certain sort of stoic acceptance both of life's pains and pleasures, will be the fulfilled man. If that is not true, then, for me, nothing is true: and this is what I try to tell the children.

This is the most conspicuous element in the ideology of children's books, and the easiest to detect. Its presence is conscious, deliberate and in some measure 'pointed', even when as with Treece there is nothing unusual or unfamiliar in the message the writer is hoping to convey.

It is at this level of intended *active ideology* that fiction carries new ideas, nonconformist or revolutionary attitudes, and efforts to change imaginative awareness in line with contemporary social criticism. This causes difficulties both for writers and critics, which can be exemplified from present-day concern with the depiction of sexual roles. There are hundreds of books that passively borrow and reproduce the sexual stereotyping they inherit from earlier fiction. No one notices, except radical adult readers (and perhaps some children) who are alert to it and offended by it. On the other hand, any novel that questions the stereotypes and sets out to reflect anti-sexist attitudes will almost inevitably do so conspicuously because it depicts surprising rather than customary behaviour. Gene Kemp's *The Turbulent Term of Tyke Tiler* achieved success by tricking the reader into assuming that the narrator was a boy, only to discover at the last gasp that she was a girl. Its astonishing effect as an anti-sexist story was largely due to its ingenious self-disguise. Much the same is true of anti-racist or anti-classist fiction. In so far as it diverges from stock assumptions about race or class, it may seem crudely didactic. If on the other hand the author seeks to present as natural a society without racial prejudice or class division and to leave out tutelary scenes of conflict, she risks blunting the ideological content and presenting happenings which readers simply do not believe. The writer faces a dilemma: it is very difficult in contemporary Britain to write an anti-sexist, anti-racist or anti-classist novel without revealing that these are still objectives, principles and ideals rather than the realities of predictable everyday behaviour.

These problems naturally mutate over time. In 2011 it seems clear that in some respects the stresses of sex, race and class have eased and improved over the last twenty years. In other ways, though, they have simply changed. For example, the problem of racial divisions has inevitably been affected by the multi-ethnic, multi-lingual immigration which recent years have seen, while traditional class differences have been displaced by money, and ever-deepening gulfs between income-rich and income-poor. Ideals and realities remain far apart. If writers present as natural and commonplace the behaviour they would *like* to be natural and commonplace, they risk muting the social effectiveness of stories. If they dramatize the social tensions, they risk a superficial ideological stridency.

The writer may opt for more circuitous methods. The more gifted the writer, the more likely to do so. If the fictional world is fully imagined and realized, it may carry its ideological burden more covertly, showing things as they are but trusting to literary organization rather than explicitly didactic guidelines to achieve a moral effect. Misunderstandings may follow if you are unlucky or too trusting. The hand of anti-racist censorship has begun to fall occasionally on the greatest anti-racist text in all literature, *Huckleberry Finn*. Twain's ideological error is to be always supremely the novelist rather than the preacher, to present his felt truth uncompromisingly rather than opt for educative adjustments to it, and to trust the intelligence of his readers. Perhaps the most luminous moment in anti-racist storytelling comes when Huck, arriving at the Phelpses' farm and being mistaken for Tom Sawyer, has to fabricate an excuse for late arrival by inventing a river-boat mishap:

> 'It warn't the grounding – that didn't keep us back but a little. We blowed out a cylinder-head.'
> 'Good gracious! anybody hurt?'
> 'No'm. Killed a nigger.'
> 'Well, it's lucky; because sometimes people do get hurt.'

This snatch of dialogue is a devastating sign of what comes naturally to Huck's mind as soon as he begins to role-play Tom, but its full effect depends on its late placing in the novel, in the wake of all we have seen already of Huck's 'sound heart and deformed conscience'. It is a crucial point: you cannot experience the book as an anti-racist text unless you know *how to read a novel*. In modern children's writing the consciously didactic text rarely displays such confidence in its readers, with the unhappy result that reformist ideological explicitness is often achieved at the cost of imaginative depth.

The inference is clear: in literature as in life the undeserved advantage lies with *passive ideology*. The second category of ideological content we must thus take into account is the individual writer's unexamined assumptions. As soon as these are admitted to be relevant, it becomes impossible to confine ideology to a writer's conscious intentions or articulated messages, and necessary to accept that all children's literature is inescapably didactic:

> Since children's literature is didactic it must by definition be a repository, in a literate society almost the quintessential source, of the values that parents and others hope to teach to the next generation. (Musgrave, *From Brown to Bunter*)

This is merely to accept what is surely obvious: writers for children (like writers for adults) cannot hide what their values are. Even if beliefs are passive and unexamined, and no part of any conscious proselytising, the texture of language and story will reveal them and communicate them. The working of ideology at this level is not incidental or unimportant. It might seem that values whose presence can only be convincingly demonstrated by an adult with some training in critical skills are unlikely to carry much potency with children. More probably the reverse is true: the values at stake are usually those which are taken for granted by the writer, and reflect the writer's integration in a society which unthinkingly accepts them. In turn this means that children, unless they are helped to notice what is there, will take them for granted too. Unexamined, passive values are widely *shared* values, and we should not underestimate the powers of reinforcement vested in quiescent and unconscious ideology.

Again I will take a pleasant example. It occurs in Richmal Crompton's *William the Bad*. Henry is summing up the salient features of British party politics before the gang hold their elections:

'There's four sorts of people tryin' to get to be rulers. They all want to make things better, but they want to make 'em better in different ways. There's Conservatives, an' they want to make things better by keepin' 'em jus' like what they are now. An' there's Liberals, an' they want to make things better by alterin' them jus' a bit, but not so's anyone'd notice, an' there's Socialists, an' they want to make things better by taken' everyone's money off 'em an' there's Communists an' they want to make things better by killin' everyone but themselves.'

This is fun, and not to be taken solemnly, but it is not exactly evenhanded fun. I do not think Miss Crompton is deliberately making propaganda, but there is not much doubt where her own sympathies lie or where she tacitly assumes that the reader's will follow. The joke about Conservatives and Liberals is a joke about *our sort*, and the joke about Socialists and Communists is a joke about a *different sort*. The interest of the example lies in the gentle, unconsidered bias of the humour. Behind it lurks an assumption of uncontroversial familiarity. It can be an instructive exercise to recast the joke, so that the bias dips in the opposite direction – suppose, for example, that the list began with 'There's Conservatives, an' they want to make things better by makin' rich people richer an' poor people poorer.' It might still be funny, but it would at once acquire a shading of aggressive propagandist intention. As a character remarks in another, later and more radical children's book, Susan Price's *From Where I Stand* :

'Ah. It'll be something left-wing, then, if *he* calls them "political" in that voice-of-doom. The Tories aren't political, you know. They just are.'

This is a very small instance, introduced simply for illustration's sake, of something present to some degree in all fiction and intrinsic to its nature. There is no act of self-censorship by which a writer can exclude or disguise the essential self. Sometimes, moreover, the conscious *active ideology* and the *passive ideology* of a novel are at odds with each other, and 'official' ideas contradicted by unconscious assumptions. Since this is by no means true of fiction only, the skills of analysis applied to different levels of a text should form part of teacher training in any society which hopes for adequate literacy. By teaching children how to develop an alert enjoyment of stories, we are also equipping them to meet linguistic malpractices of more consequential kinds.

To associate the ideology of children's books with ideology in its broader definitions, we need to consider the third dimension of its presence. This is the one to which developments in literary theory, by now familiar and widely accepted, have introduced us, and the one from which domestic skirmishing between book people and child people has tended to distract our attention. In order to affirm its general nature, I take a convenient summary of its position from a study not of children's literature but of sixteenth-century poetry:

> How does ideology affect literary texts? The impact of ideology upon the writings of a particular society – or, for that matter, on the conventions and strategies by which we read those writings – is no different from the way it influences any other cultural practice. In no case, in Macherey's words, does the writer, as the producer of the text, manufacture the materials with which he works. The power of ideology is inscribed within the words, the rule-systems, and codes which constitute the text. Imagine ideology as a powerful force hovering over us as we read a text; as we read it reminds us of what is correct, commonsensical, or 'natural'. It tries, as it were, to guide both the writing and our subsequent readings of a text into coherence. When a text is written, ideology works to make some things more natural to write; when a text is read, it works to conceal struggles and repressions, to force language into conveying only those meanings reinforced by the dominant forces of our society. (Gary Waller, *English Poetry of the Sixteenth Century*)

If this is true, as I believe it is, we must think in terms that include but also transcend the idea of individual authorship, and reappraise the relationship between the author and the reader. In the case of children's literature, our thinking may be affected by an over-simplified stereotype of possible authority and influence. The

41

individual writer is likely, as we have seen, to make conscious choices about the explicit ideology of his work, while the uniqueness of imaginative achievements rests on the private, unrepeatable configurations writers make at subconscious level from the common stock of their experience.

Our habit is so much to cherish individualism, however, that we often overlook the huge commonalities of an age, and the captivity of mind we undergo by living in our own time and place and no other. A large part of any book is written not by its author but by the world its author lives in. To accept the point one has only to recognize the rarity of occasions when a writer manages to recolour the meaning of a single word: almost all the time we are the acquiescent prisoners of other people's meanings. As a rule, writers for children are transmitters not of themselves uniquely but of the worlds they share.

The familiar term for this phenomenon is *zeitgeist*, or 'spirit of the age', but in this context I would prefer to call it '*organic ideology*', and it is best explained by an analogy which will distinguish it from *active ideology* and *passive ideology*. The most obvious analogy is with the human body.

Each of us has one. In a manner equivalent to *active ideology*, we decide in our own best interests what to do with it. We use it to play football or netball or climb mountains or drive a car, or to perform or avoid performing manual work in order to feed it. Each of these activities entails deliberately changing its capacities from those it has at its beginning, and through its lifetime of learning and practice we make innumerable conscious choices. (I ignore but recognize that the brain which makes the choices is itself a part of the organism, just as the active ideology of literature can only be devised by an educated biological intelligence.)

In a manner equivalent to *passive ideology*, we service our bodies in ways shared with every other human being, taking for granted that we eat, drink, defecate, sleep and indeed breathe. Much as we may routinely enjoy these taken-for-granted matters, they only become a major conscious concern when they go wrong or are denied to us.

But at the third level, equivalent to *organic ideology*, larger forces are at work. Our bodies change, sometimes rapidly and obviously, sometimes so slowly that we scarcely notice. They get bigger (and eventually a little smaller). At puberty they develop exciting and disturbing new features, usually with our pleasurable consent but without our permission. They grow older. They grow old. They are always on the move, as is organic ideology. And eventually, whatever efforts we make to postpone the event, they die. Similarly, the organic ideology of the world we live in changes and dies. We may re-imagine the organic ideology which ruled our forefathers, but we can never reoccupy it. Sometimes we can pinpoint an exact instant of bodily or ideological organic change, but often, like the onset of slow terminal illness, its arrival is gradual, inconspicuous, and unnoticed. Noticed or not, it seeps irresistibly into language, the way we write and the way we read.

For modern children's writing this has many implications, but I would pick out two. First, the writer's ability to reshape his world is strictly limited. It is in his power (and may be his duty) to recommend an improved world, reflecting not what it is but what he hopes it might be. But this undertaking is bound by the same constraint as the literature of warning, which depicts a corrupted world as the author fears it truly is or might be. The starting point for each must be a shared understanding of the present, and an actuality which the young reader believes in.

The second point is that we may live in a period when our common ideology has many local fractures, so that children in different parts of the same national society are caught between bonding and difference. If children who are citizens of one country live in worlds within a world, discrete subcultures within a culture, they will need different storytelling voices to speak to them – voices which can speak within an ideology which for them is coherent and complete. As I hope this discussion has indicated, ideology is inseparable from language, and divergences of language within a national culture point to divisions and fragmentations in its shared ideology. In Britain as in other countries there is indeed a common national language, but when that is said it must be qualified. Britain is also a country of many languages apart from English and of many Englishes, and the children who speak them ideally need both a common national literature and local literatures which speak to and for themselves. Robert Leeson makes this point in his case for 'alternative' publishing for children. He begins by referring specifically to the spoken language and to dialect.

The very richness of non-standard English is in itself a challenge to the whole system of education and literature, but a challenge that must be met. London schools at the moment are grappling (or not grappling) with new streams of language like Creole.

He goes on to argue that 'alternative' publications need not be subject to the orthodox scrutiny of critics 'provided [they] can meet the critical response of [their] readers'. Interestingly he then goes on to make two significant conflations of ideas: first, he associates linguistic and literary subcultures with the literature of 'progressive' values, and second, he associates alternative publishing of books *for* children with publishing of books *by* children.

So far the alternative publishers have not made great inroads into the field of fiction for the young. There have been some feminist stories for small children, some teenage writings, original and re-told folk stories from ethnic minorities. These are modest beginnings.

The point which is half made here can be fully understood in its general implications if we define 'ideology' largely and precisely enough. The two points are crucial: subcultures of language are inseparable from the climate of ideas and values at work in them, and children inhabiting a subculture need to create a literature of their own, not merely be supplied with one. Leeson's ideas on this point are important and helpful but unnecessarily restricted in their scope. Like many other commentators, he is in practice most concerned with the London community of ethnic minorities and progressive groups. Such critics tend to write as if other places, other social groupings, other sites of active dialects, other schemes of ethical values did not exist, or had no comparable needs. If our thinking about ideology is clear enough, it is apparent that the same considerations apply to *all* children in any part of society (and in practice this probably means all parts of society) where there is tension between a common ideology and local circumstances. To appreciate the implications for children's literature demands acceptance that we do indeed inhabit a fragmented society, where each of the fragments needs and deserves to feel a confident sense of its value. As Leeson argues – but with a wider inference than he draws from it – we need a national children's literature (not to mention an international one) but also local literatures for particular racial or regional or social or (why not?) sexual groups, and also a literature made by the children themselves. Only when we have a coherent definition of ideology does this become adequately clear.

The reader as ideologist

Above all, it emerges from this argument that ideology is not something that is transferred to children as if they were empty receptacles. It is something they already possess, having drawn it from a mass of experiences far more powerful than literature.

In literature, as in life, we have to start from where children are, and with their own (often inarticulate) ideology. This offends some commentators, who prefer the literature to begin where they wish children were, or assume that easy transformations can be made by humanely open-minded critical inquiry, whether based in classrooms or elsewhere. Rob Grunsell, describing his experiences in running an alternative school for chronic truants in London, reports the discomfiting consequences of moving too rationally and openly beyond a pre-existent teenage ideology:

> At lunch they had opinions in plenty, particularly about the blacks and the Pakis. It seemed to me such an obvious place to start, so I planned out a lesson on racial attitudes – a straight survey of what they thought, with no judgements and no 'right' answers. They designed the questionnaire with me, enjoying filling in their answers. From that point on it was a disaster. The answers weren't the same. 'Was Jimmy right?', why were they wrong? I couldn't convince them, because they couldn't listen, that there were no right answers. Here, in a lesson, hating Pakis because they're 'dim' and 'chicken' was obviously wrong. They sensed what I thought, even though I hadn't said it. They had lost, as usual, and more hopelessly than usual since they could do nothing about it. My prize-winning lesson in open-ended exploratory learning produced five miserable, depressed people.

A similar result is produced by much over-confident and unconcealed didacticism in modern children's books, as it is by much persuasive rationality in classroom discussion. Where the ideology is explicit, it does not matter how morally unanswerable the substance is if it speaks persuasively only to those who are persuaded already, leaving others with their own divergent ideology intensified by resentful bemusement. Susan Price's *From Where I Stand*, which I referred to earlier, is passionately anti-racist, operating very much at the level of conscious authorial intention. At one point a highly intelligent Bangladeshi teenager, Kamla, is interviewed by the headmistress of her comprehensive school about an anti-racist pamphlet she has helped to compose. The headmistress tries to reason with her:

> 'You are going to tell me that Asian and black children are often teased and bullied by white children in this school. This isn't news to me, you know. I am quite aware of it. Whenever I can, I intervene, I punish children who are caught bullying or robbing others – but I punish them for bullying, for blackmail, for theft, not for racism. You see, it isn't always wise to tackle these things head on, my dear; I wonder if you can understand that? These attitudes are entrenched. Unfortunately, many of the children here have parents who are racist in their views. In that case, if you attack the opinion, then you attack the parents, and you are telling the children that their parents are bad people – now, that doesn't help. It only antagonizes them, reinforces their beliefs . . . And they are only *children*, Kamla.'

Susan Price's storytelling is very skilfully organized to discredit the headmistress by presenting her as one who is at best evasive and negligent in her efforts to subdue racist behaviour, and at worst has racist sympathies herself. The speech quoted above is thus placed in a context designed to undermine it. Readers are intended to conclude that the reasons for inaction given in the last sentences – reasons put forward often by real teachers in the real world – are merely disreputable rationalizations of unprincipled tolerance, if not something worse, with the implication that such reasons usually are. Susan Price is using literary skills to checkmate her opponents in an ideological chess game. But in the imperfect world these are genuine problems for teachers who try to educate children in anti-racist morality. It is unfortunately true that well-disposed ideological enthusiasm can be counter-productive in school classrooms; and it can be likewise in stories. So the likely effect of Susan Price's storytelling is to deepen children's entrenched attitudes, good and bad alike. If it were not so, the stresses on our social fabric would be a great deal easier to deal with.

Locating the ideology of individual books

I have argued, therefore, that we should accept both the omnipresence of ideology and the realities of fragmentation, divergence, passivity, inertia, conservatism, invisibility, unreasoningness, resistance and sheer incomprehension in much of its expression and reception by the author and the child. Although it is easiest to illustrate the ideological process from the repertoire of *active* ideology in progressive modern fiction, that is only because didactic content is more obtrusive there, not because it is present on a larger scale than it is in traditional fiction. On all sides, in numerous commentaries on children's fiction (not to mention many novels themselves) a customary error is to make the wrong implicit analogy, by treating ideology as if it were a political policy, when in fact it is a climate of belief. The first can be changed, and itemized, and imposed, and legislated into reality and (though not always!) vindicated by pure reason. The second is vague, and holistic, and pliant, and unstable, and can only evolve.

The first priority is to understand how the ideology of any given book can be located. Above all, such an understanding is important for teachers, especially primary school teachers and English specialists. Their task is to teach children how to read, so that to the limits of each child's capacity that child will not be at the mercy of *what* she reads. I shall conclude, then, with some examples of the kind of question which teachers in training might usefully be taught to ask about children's books, in order to clarify the ideology at work in them. They are mostly questions which adults generally might find interesting in order to test their own recreational fiction, and which can easily be modified for use in classrooms. The purpose, as I have tried to indicate throughout, is a modest one: not to evaluate, discredit or applaud a writer's ideology, but simply to see what it is.

The questions are only examples, and teachers and others will readily be able to augment them.

1. What happens if the components of a text are transposed or reversed (as I suggested might be done with Richmal Crompton's political joke in *William the Bad*)? Does examination of the negative, so to speak, show unsuspected blights in the published picture? In particular, do we observe that a book that seems to be asserting a principle is only attacking a symptom? Is this 'anti-sexist novel' in fact sexist itself, and merely anti-male? Does this war story attack the Germans for atrocities that are approved when the British inflict them?

2. Consider the denouements of some books, and the happy (or unhappy) ending. Does the happy ending of a novel amount to a 'contract of reaffirmation' of questionable values which have earlier seemed to be on trial? Is the conclusion imaginatively coherent, or does it depend on implicit assumptions which are at odds with the active ideology? Are there any loose ends (not so much of plot but of thought and feeling)? (Although it is not a children's book, students may find a particularly interesting example in the closing paragraphs of Richard Hughes's *A High Wind in Jamaica*.) If some 'happy endings' reconverge on the dominant ideology, is it also true that an unhappy ending is a device for denying such reconvergence, and hence for reinforcing a blend of ideological and emotional protest? (Students might consider the brilliantly effective unhappy endings of Susan Price's *Twopence a Tub* and Jan Mark's *Divide and Rule*.)

3. Are the values of a novel shown as a 'package' in which separate items appear to interlock? For example, does one story condemn racial prejudice and social class prejudice as if they were automatically interdependent, and does another in the same way celebrate a seemingly inseparable threesome made up of patriotism, courage and personal loyalty? (Biggles books are a good source of study on 'packaging' of various kinds.) Are these groups of virtues or vices necessarily or logically connected with each other? Are they being grouped together in order to articulate some larger, aggregated

virtue or vice, such as 'white Britishness'? Students may find it interesting to bring this exercise to bear comparatively on the work of W.E. Johns and some current socially progressive fiction. Is it in fact a mark of quality in a book that it differentiates its values rather than fusing them in composite and (perhaps fraudulently) homogeneous groups?

4. Is it a noticeable feature of some major 'classic' children's books that they test and undermine some of the values they superficially appear to be celebrating? (I think it is. Students may find it interesting to perform this experimental inquiry on *Treasure Island*, *The Wind in the Willows*, and *Stalky and Co*, as well as *Tom Sawyer* and *Huckleberry Finn*.) Are there any modern children's books which seem to work in similar ways? Readers may find, for example, that the novels of John Christopher (notably *Fireball*) and Peter Dickinson (notably *Healer*) are more complex than they seem.

There is an important general point here. As studies based in modern critical theory have convincingly shown, many major works will sustain more radical and subversive readings than we are accustomed to. Critiques of children's literature that concentrate on active and explicit ideology tend to ignore such possibilities. They observe only the external conservative values detectable in some major children's books, and overlook the radical questioning to which the text exposes them. The fallacy (as I have earlier suggested in the case of *Huckleberry Finn*) often lies in treating the novel as if it were some other kind of writing, and so ignoring narrative procedures which are basic to its meanings. If critics can make such mistakes, so can children: they need our help in learning how to read. But that is no excuse for suppressing or reclassifying the books.

5. Are desirable values associated with niceness of character, and vice versa? Is it really true that a given attractive philosophy or action could not believably be held or performed by someone whose character was in other ways unpleasant? How much allowance is there (and how much should there be in a children's book) for inconsistency, or for dissonance between ideology and temperament? How far is a book's ideology conveyed by 'moral symmetry' in character delineation?

6. Does anyone in a story have to make a difficult *choice* – of behaviour, loyalties, values, etc. – in which there is more than one defensible course of action? Or does the plot hinge merely on a predetermined choice, and interest depend on whether or not it is successfully carried out?

7. Is any character shown as performing a mixture of roles, especially roles with sharply differentiated contexts of friendship, safety or prestige? Does any character belong as an accepted member in more than one subculture or group, and move without stress between them? If any character does so, is one such group presented by the author as deserving higher value than another? The groups may be as simple as school (both staff and peer group) and family. They may, on the other hand, extend to differences of race, culture, religion, political affiliation and social custom, as they do for example in *Kim*. *Kim* is an excellent text for students to consider, not least because it exposes the need for caution in using the vocabulary of political judgement, in this case 'racist', as a generalizing critical terminology.

8. Last and most important in this selection is the question of omission and invisibility. Who are the people who 'do not exist' in a given story? This may mean people who are present but humanly downgraded, as if inscribed above the writer's desk were the words 'All human beings are human, but some are more human than others.' Downgraded groups include servants, but may also in a given case include teachers, or even parents. More seriously, they may include criminals and policemen. More seriously still, they may include foreigners, soldiers, girls, women and blacks. Arguably most seriously of all (given its long and appalling history) they may include people who subscribe, or do not subscribe, to a particular religious belief. These last groups are more serious invisibilities because they do not plausibly represent mere story conventions but curtailments of humanity embedded in an ideology.

Omission takes many forms: for example, the performance of important life-supporting tasks for children without any reference to the workers (such as mothers) who carry them out. Invisibility may take many forms, for example, the denial of names, the identification of people by what they do rather than what they are, and the absorption of individuals into social and racial groups. It can be helpful again to take an 'adult' text before considering children's books with students, and the most rewarding one I know to introduce this inquiry is Conrad's *Heart of Darkness*.

Taken together, questions such as these may serve effectively to lift ideology 'off the page' and bring it from obscure and unexpected places into the light, but it need not and should not suppress the uniqueness of individual stories, or convert them into cadavers for pedagogic dissection or for classroom autopsy. What we call 'ideology', as I have tried to argue, is a living thing, and something we need to know as we need to know ourselves. Very much like that, because it is a part of us.

Ideology in Practice:
E. Nesbit's *The Railway Children*

In the previous chapter I set out a case for taking the ideology of children's fiction seriously, as part of a general mission by teachers, parents and others to help children to become effective readers. By 'effective' I mean readers who are alert to what is happening in written (and spoken) language, and what ideologies they are being invited to accept and share. In the simplest terms, these are made up of three components: the beliefs or attitudes that a writer consciously sets out to transmit (active ideology); those that are not knowingly voiced but creep into the text unawares (passive ideology); and those that are neither consciously nor unconsciously personal to the writer but are part of the ideological air that everyone is breathing at the time and place of writing (organic ideology). I also emphasized that every reading is a negotiation and reciprocal exchange, since all readers, including children, bring to the text their own armoury of conscious and hidden ideological predispositions.

In arguing this case, and suggesting ways in which the ideology of fictions might be discovered and exposed, I referred to a number of children's books to illustrate specific points. It seems worthwhile to follow up the general argument by looking now in detail at a single specific text, and see what happens when it is opened up more intimately than any reader, whether professional critic or child, would normally set out to do.

My purpose, so to speak, is to examine ideology in slow motion. In so far as I can show that they are present in the language of a story, these will be matters that every alert reader will register and be affected by, usually without realizing it, in the normal-speed business of reading. But in so far as I seem to be finding what the reader of this chapter is not convinced is there, it may be my own ideology, and not the author's, which is coming into view. Everything that follows, therefore, is about the nature of a literary work, but also about the practice of reading.

Choosing a text

The book I have chosen to explore is E. Nesbit's *The Railway Children* (1905). These are my reasons for choosing it.

– I needed a children's novel that is, or seems to be, quite simple, and appears to carry an uncomplicated and quite open active ideology.

– The book should be readily accessible. Although the following discussion is meant to be free-standing and self-explanatory – hence the inclusion of a plot summary – it is obviously important that readers who wish to can easily set my reading against their own. *The Railway Children* has been almost continuously in print since it was published, and is widely available.

– I looked for a so-called 'classic' text, one which is so familiar that it is taken for granted, and has what might be called an 'inheritance of affection', which children coming to it freshly soon perceive. *The Railway Children* certainly meets this criterion, as is clear when it is transposed to another medium. The book was made into a classic children's film in 1970, which was and still is popular. More recently, it has been ingeniously staged, to seemingly universal delight, on actual railway platforms with a full-size vintage locomotive in the cast – first at the National Railway Museum in York, and then at the former Eurostar Terminal at Waterloo Station in London.

– I wanted a story neither written nor set in the present day, but narrating events and situations that have clear modern equivalents. Absent fathers and one-parent families are modern commonplaces. Sudden falls from prosperity to adversity and their eventual correction are a staple of storytelling at all times. Children who show initiative, behave courageously, and succeed where adults have failed are a stereotype of children's fiction. *The Railway Children* can be represented as composed of nothing but storytelling clichés, except that it is often Nesbit's own considerable influence that has made them so. In essence, the action is not out of date a century later.

On the other hand, the hundred-year gap allows the ideology to stand out more clearly than it does in a modern text. There are things that Nesbit takes for granted that are obsolete in our world and therefore conspicuous; conversely, we may not recognize when she is being subversive because what was daring in Edwardian England is normal and accepted now. Neither her active nor her passive ideology will be the same as ours. We cannot of course re-enter the Edwardian climate of belief, though we can re-imagine it. (A.S. Byatt's novel *The Children's Book*, in which a fictionalized E. Nesbit is a major character, is a *tour de force* of historical imagination.) But the distance of time may make us more aware of its ideological climate than we are of the one that we ourselves inhabit.

Of course a story of such ostensible simplicity as *The Railway Children* may reveal no such complexities as these, but if it does it is a timely indication that in terms of ideology there is no such thing as a simple text.

There are other reasons for selecting Nesbit as a focus for close study, and *The Railway Children* in particular. This is her most naturalistic children's novel. Although it is set in a society and world so radically unlike ours, it somehow manages not to appear deterrently 'old-fashioned'. In part, as I have suggested, this is due to the sturdy longevity of its plot devices, but is also explained by Nesbit's presentation of the central three child characters. They may seem young for their age by modern standards, and very innocent, but Nesbit may have hoped for this response in her child readers: several times she addresses the reader directly and conspiratorially, as someone shrewd and knowing, able to see through events and anticipate outcomes as the children themselves cannot. Moreover, their behaviour is generally convincing. Clearly the children are not 'streetwise' – they do after all live in a world without streets! Nesbit's ear for speech and dialogue is one of her great strengths, and while the passage of a hundred years inevitably makes some of their talk sound dated, it is remarkable how modern much of it remains. Their immaturity may still seem problematic, but one factor mitigates this for the present-day reader. Not only is Nesbit a sharp observer of children's behaviour when supposedly unobserved (a writerly skill often attributed to

Nesbit's own failure ever to grow up) but she accurately registers a differential speech, depending on whether the children are talking among themselves or to adults, and with it a differential behaviour, which fluctuates between the childish bickering of private quarrels and the leaps of maturity evident in their reactions to emergencies.

The instabilities of childness represented here are true of children in all times and places, and largely cancel out the different expectations linked to actual chronological age. Not all adult readers would necessarily give Nesbit credit for these qualities, but there appears to be broad agreement about them, and they account for her status in a number of critical discussions as the founding modern children's writer.

Thus Julia Briggs begins her admirable standard life of Nesbit with exactly that claim. 'E. Nesbit is the first modern writer for children. She invented the children's adventure story more or less single-handed.' Alison Lurie, in *Don't Tell the Grown-Ups: Subversive Children's Literature*, agrees: 'it is possible now to speak of juvenile literature as before or after E. Nesbit', and 'Every writer of children's fantasy since Nesbit's time is indebted to her.' *The Railway Children* is not, at least in the conventional sense, a fantasy, but the same claim can be made for her influence on the family adventure story. Humphrey Carpenter, who dislikes Nesbit, feels grudgingly obliged to make the same concession: 'She is an author whose methods are comparatively easy to copy, and many have done so, though whether to the ultimate benefit of children's literature seems questionable.'

For all these reasons, *The Railway Children* seems to me an ideal text for a close study of ideology in practice.

The story

Although *The Railway Children* is quite easy to find, for the convenience of readers I now include an outline summary of the story.

The railway children are Roberta (usually called Bobbie) whose twelfth birthday comes in the story, Peter, who is ten, and Phyllis, about eight. They are a middle-class family whose father works for the government, and they live in an extremely comfortable villa in suburban London. They have a cook and other maids to serve them. Both parents are child-orientated, loving and attentive, and family life takes precedence over social life. This domestic idyll collapses suddenly when Father is arrested, unjustly accused of spying for the Russians. He is convicted and imprisoned. The children know only that he has gone away. Much later in the story Bobbie, and only Bobbie, accidentally uncovers the hidden truth about their plight.

Mother and the children are forced to leave London and material prosperity behind. They travel by train, preceded by their essential belongings, to an isolated house near a country village, where they arrive in the night, tired and hungry, to find that the expected meal is missing. Mother and the children cope overnight with practical resilience, and in the morning things seem better.

What especially makes things better for the children is that they are living near the railway. Soon they are waving to passing trains, and from one train an Old Gentleman regularly waves back. This greeting is the first, and ultimately crucial, friendship that the children make in their new environment. But life is hard. They are now poor. Mother writes stories to earn a living, and no longer has time to spend with them, so they are left largely to themselves. The focus of their lives becomes the railway.

Their first railway adventure is disastrous. Peter sets out to replenish their meagre fuel supplies by 'mining', that is stealing, coal from the station yard. He is caught by the Stationmaster, but escapes with nothing worse than a lecture. Thereafter they have a series of further railway adventures. They prevent an accident by warning an approaching train after a landslide, they rescue a boy who is injured in the railway tunnel during a school run, and they awaken a sleeping signalman just in time. They also befriend Perks, the station porter, and through him other villagers. By way of variation they rescue a baby from a fire on a canal boat, and in consequence befriend the barge community as well. Meanwhile mother lives a hardworking and reclusive life, avoiding the village and making occasional mysterious journeys. The children, Bobbie especially, take their own initiatives to deal with household crises, and to assist a destitute and ailing Russian refugee. The Old Gentleman is several times instrumental in helping them, and his intervention is finally crucial in bringing about their father's exoneration and release. The family know nothing of this until Bobbie happens to be on the station when the train arrives that brings him home, and the family is reunited.

Perspectives on a simple story

The Railway Children is not exactly *Hamlet*, and it might seem that there is little scope for different readings of such a straightforward tale. But this is not so. Here are three.

Humphrey Carpenter's *Secret Gardens: A Study of the Golden Age of Children's Literature* is mainly a study of fantasy for children in Victorian and Edwardian England. But he does not value fantasy for its own sake, rather for what it can do, and what it can do is encourage children to look critically and at times iconoclastically at adults and the adult world; to become mature themselves, and to see 'real life' as it really is. The period's fantasy, he says, 'dealt largely with utopias, and posited the existence of Arcadian societies remote from the nature and concerns of the everyday world; yet in doing this it was commenting, often satirically and critically, on real life.' Clearly in Carpenter's view this is also what it should be doing, and Edith Nesbit was not. Nesbit falls short in her novels generally, he argues, by presenting the adult as a 'kindly protector'. In *The Treasure Seekers* 'There is not one sharp or satirical portrait of an adult', and 'The truth is that Nesbit was essentially a late Victorian writer, who accepted the attitude, prevalent in the 1870s and 1880s, that children are delightfully naïve.'

The Railway Children, as a purportedly naturalistic novel, stirs Carpenter to be particularly scathing.

> [Roberta] and her brother and sister are quite unable to comprehend, despite every kind of hint, that their father is in prison. Nesbit keeps them in ignorance partly to achieve the book's climax, but also, one feels, *because she likes to shelter children from the real world* [my italics]. The story . . . ducks out of what might have been its real issues – the children's discovery of the possibility of gross injustice in the adult world . . . and does not allow them to experience any real hardships during their supposed poverty . . . Instead Nesbit contents herself with a series of soap-opera crises . . . The only concession to reality is a rather sentimental account of the family helping a political prisoner.

There are valid and interesting points here, which I shall address later. But I need to draw attention straight away to

Carpenter's repeated use of the words 'real' and 'reality', and his complaint that Nesbit is sheltering her readers. Far from pioneering a new twentieth-century children's literature, Nesbit as Carpenter sees her is a superannuated Victorian peddling a regressive view of childhood.

Set this against Alison Lurie's view in *Don't Tell the Grown-Ups*. I have already noted her belief that Nesbit was a pivotal figure, a marker for the start of modern children's writing. She was also, for Lurie, a radical and trailblazing thinker. 'Nesbit was the first to write at length for children as intellectual equals and in their own language. Her books were startlingly innovative in other ways: they took place in contemporary England and recommended socialist solutions to its problems; they presented a modern view of childhood.' Among Nesbit's modernist ideas, one in particular stands out, and will emerge later as markedly important in the ideology of *The Railway Children*: 'One especially radical, and at the time highly subversive, feature of Nesbit's tales is her implicit feminism. Her books are full of girls who are as brave and adventurous as their brothers.' Lurie thus sees the book in terms of active ideology, of which she in turn actively approves.

In the light of what comes later, I wish to emphasize the link that Lurie makes between feminism and bravery. Lurie's conclusion could hardly be more at odds with Carpenter's: she concludes that Nesbit 'managed not only to create some of the best children's books ever written, but to quietly popularize ideas about society and about childhood that were, in her time, extremely subversive.'

In his study *The Promise of Happiness* Fred Inglis finds something different again. Inglis is by temperament a traditional liberal with socialist convictions; and he is an optimist, who believes in the achievable improvement of society and the role of children's literature in encouraging children to be positive and ambitious in their hopes for human betterment. It naturally follows that his readings of children's books are most concerned with active ideology. In his Preface he declares his interest in 'the way these particular forms of the social imagination [i.e. children's books] try to fix admired social values in a story, give them place and name and continuity'. The best children's books for him have a palpable design upon children, albeit a benevolent one. He refers to the 'strenuous highmindedness' of *The Railway Children*, which he suggests 'may sometimes become irksome'. (So it may, if indeed you find it there. This seems to me quite an arduous job, since it requires you to ignore Nesbit's sense of humour.) This approach eventually leads Inglis to something central to his own convictions and undeniably important in the novel – the exceptional prevalence of altruism. He says:

> In *The Railway Children*, the old gentleman represents the possibility of a prompt and rational altruism, the possibility, even the likelihood, of which we would always seek to urge upon children. Odd though it now sounds to say so, it is the dream hidden in the idea of a welfare state . . .
> It is important in the simple moral patterning of the novel that the children, upheld by the altruism of so many people – old gentleman, railwayman, doctor – which their own earnest commitment to goodness may be said to have called out, themselves go on to act philanthropically [in the birthday present collection for Mr Perks].

In terms of ideology, once again there are no simple books and no simple readers. Each of these three critics has brought to bear an ideology *of* the children's book in order to discover (or in Carpenter's case complainingly fail to) a complementary ideology *in* the children's book. For Carpenter the children's book (not least in fantasy) is a maturing encounter with 'real life', and does not seek to protect the reader from its darker aspects. For him *The Railway Children* fails to offer this. For Lurie the most interesting children's book is radical and subversive, and subversion is duly there in Nesbit. For Inglis the good children's book is consciously an optimistic moral and political invitation, and *The Railway Children* issues one.

In this chapter and the last I try to be as objective as possible, while knowing that total objectivity is out of reach. Every reader is an ideologist.

Exploring the text

I shall now examine first a single incident, one which raises quite varied questions that illustrate the difficulties of finding safe ideological ground, especially when a book is not (as all books quickly cease to be) contemporary with the reader. This will introduce a series of enquiries into the main ideological issues raised by Nesbit's novel.

i. *Peter and the coal*

Apart from waving at the trains, the children's first close encounter with the railway is Peter's exploit as a coal-miner. Coal stocks at the Three Chimneys are low, and Mother has decreed that fires in June are forbidden, even on cold days. Peter sets out to remedy the situation by 'mining' the coal stocks at the station. He knows quite well that this 'may be wrong', but fantasizes his way out of moral consciousness and guilt by his imaginative role-play as a 'miner'. Alas, this cuts no ice with the Station Master when Peter is caught black-handed in the act of theft. The Station Master succinctly does two things. He makes the moral issue tersely clear in a single sentence, and he lets Peter off with a warning:

> 'I'll tell you what I'll do. I'll look over it this once. But you remember, young gentleman, stealing is stealing, and what's mine isn't yours, whether you call it mining or whether you don't. Run along home.'

The problem is this. What view should we take of the Station Master's clemency?

To the modern reader this may seem simple. This is petty theft, and nowadays, even if police were summoned, the worst that could befall Peter would be a caution, which is effectively what he gets. But here is a report from the *Yorkshire Evening Press* in April 1910, five years after *The Railway Children* was published:

> The twelve-year-old boy Charles Bulbeck who had been sentenced to six strokes with the birch and six years' detention in a training ship for stealing 5d worth of coal [2p in modern currency] was, by the order of the Home Secretary, Mr Churchill, restored to his parents at Aldbourne, Sussex. Interviewed at his home the boy said: 'On Monday I walked to the police court, ever so many miles, because my father had not enough money to pay for me and him to go by train. I was very frightened in the dock,

and after the terrible birching blood ran. A policeman took me to Portslade on the train, and when I got out of the station I had to walk to the school, a mile and a half uphill. I felt ready to drop. I had to be bathed, and they cut my hair short and fitted me in reformatory clothes. I had no food from 7-30 a.m. till five o'clock, when we had tea. At the school everybody was most kind to me'.

Churchill's intervention clearly indicates that this savage punishment was even in 1910 regarded as excessive and perversely harsh, as does the boy's reception at the school. But the incident puts Peter's 'mining' in perspective. He steals more coal than this boy did, and though he repeats his mother's claim that they are 'too poor to have a fire', they are not so poor that Mother cannot afford train journeys. The Station Master is being very lenient indeed. Why?

There seem to be four possible explanations, different in kind. It may be that the episode reflects Nesbit's acquiescence in the social divisions of her time. Peter (unlike Charles Bulbeck) is a middle-class boy, a 'young gentleman', as the Station Master says in mid-rebuke. His first reaction when he recognizes Peter is an immediate change of tone.

'Why,' said he, 'you're the children from the Three Chimneys up yonder. So nicely dressed, too. Tell me now, what made you do such a thing?' . . . He spoke much more gently now . . .

Nesbit then may be subscribing unthinkingly to the social norms of her time, and is thus governed by her passive ideology. This is much the likeliest explanation, though it may be concurrent with others. More speculatively, it may be that she is indeed subverting socio-legal norms, and promulgating a milder, more humane response to petty delinquency than was customary, even if the norm was gentler than that experienced by poor Charles Bulbeck. In that case active ideology determines the event. On the other hand, she may as a novelist be setting the stage for the benevolent society that the children will experience, on the railway and elsewhere, throughout the book: the idealized world of reciprocal kindness and altruism that Fred Inglis commends. Or perhaps as an author she is doing exactly what arouses Carpenter's displeasure, protecting the child reader from hard realities. All these possibilities are in play, and different levels of ideology may be simultaneously involved in what seems like a single reassuring incident.

ii) *Altruism*

Certainly the Station Master's leniency sets a precedent for virtually unbroken mutual goodwill and altruism between the family and the local community throughout. As yet the Station Master scarcely knows them: they are just a respectable family of incomers. Does he even know their name?

The question is pertinent. If Mr Gills knows their surname, it is more than we do. We do not know the old gentleman's name, either, and at the start of the final chapter Nesbit declines to reveal it. 'I must be allowed to keep one secret', she says. 'It's the only one; I have told you everything else.' This is an authorial fib. She has in fact gone to some lengths to hide the children's surname from us. In Chapter VII, when they enlist the old gentleman's help in tracing Mr Szezcpansky's family, he asks questions about them, 'and out came their names and ages – their Father's name and business ... and a great deal more.' To him, but not to us. (This revelation is in fact the start of the old gentleman's effort to put right the injustice done to Father.) But it is inconceivable that he would not know their names already. Only four pages earlier, in his presence they have been presented with watches to commemorate their saving of the train, and each watch is 'engraved after the name of the watch's new owner'. But only the new owners' Christian names are known to us.

Why? Common sense dictates that their surname would be locally known. Nesbit makes much of Mother posting her correspondence elsewhere, not in the village Post Office, presumably to hide a prison address; but the delivery of post, not its dispatch, would show their names, and the postman calls. It would appear that Nesbit hides their name from us to make it plausible that the villagers do not know it, either.

And if they did? If the Station Master knew that Peter was the son of a convicted traitor? We have already heard Ruth the parlour-maid's response to Peter's practical joke while they were still in

London: 'you'll go where your precious Father's gone, so I tell you straight!' What then would be the likely response of Mr Gills to Peter the coal-thief if not just his social class but family identity were known?

Usually it is the names of minor, disregarded, functional humans that are omitted. Here it is the most important surnames in the book which Nesbit hides. Clearly it is important to Nesbit that readers should accept the children's anonymity where their Father is concerned. Until Bobbie (and the old gentleman) belatedly find out the truth, no one except Mother knows it. If the villagers knew their identity, it is beyond belief that the family would be treated as they are.

So Nesbit's narrative subterfuge is essential to a primary ideology of the book: the reciprocity of altruism. The children approach the railway workers, the villagers, the old gentleman, the doctor, and even after an initial blip the bargeman, with open-hearted candour, trust and friendship, and are duly rewarded. They ask, and are given what they ask for. They behave selflessly in emergencies, and are treated selflessly in return. They give, and receive. Their innocence, derived perhaps less from immaturity than from protected lives, releases a kind of innocence in adults, freeing them from the fetters of societal habit and constraint, as witness Perks's birthday. The local result is almost a miniature social utopia.

This may be open to Carpenter's accusation of out-of-date authorial protectiveness towards the reader, or it may show idealism that defies belief. Certainly it is an optimistic ideological construct (Dennis Butts suggests that the novel's lasting popularity is due to its optimism) and places a naturalistic story on the borderline of fantasy, but it is remarkably convincing. It remains so even though Nesbit cheekily has it both ways, and at the end, when Father is vindicated, implies (for instance in the draper's boy's new-found politeness) that the locals have known the truth all along.

iii) *Class, poverty and charity*
If the ideals of social intercourse generated by the children were complete and uncontested, the novel would indeed beggar belief. In terms of plot the children's outlook is certainly victorious: it is their

(in practice Bobbie's) independent humanist initiatives and confidence in people that directly cause the incidental triumphs and the happy ending. But the book speaks with two voices. The children on the one hand are a blueprint for a new humanity (consistent with the socialist ideals of Nesbit's own political background), but on the other they are innocent and naïve children, creating a small commonweal out of a harsh, less hospitable wider world. In a letter of 1884, quoted by Julia Briggs, Nesbit had written this about the socialist Fabian Society, which dominated her family's social circle: 'There are two distinct elements in the F.S. The practical and the visionary – the first being much the strongest – but a perpetual warfare goes on between the parties... We belong – needs say – to the practical party.' The children, essentially Bobbie, are practical visionaries. They subdue class difference by ignoring it. The climax of this comes just before the end, when Bobbie is at the station, little knowing that her father's train is due, and says to Perks: 'we love you quite as much as if you were an uncle of ours'.

But there are adult practicalities as well. As we have seen, the Station Master's kindliness to Peter hinges on class awareness. In Chapter VI, when Perks is offended because no one has confided in him about the Russian prisoner, the problem is that Mother has been down to tell the Station Master all about it, and Perks was excluded. The professional class differences of status on the railway merge with Perks's consciousness of broader class division, so Mother is resentfully termed ''er Ladyship'.

Essentially it is Mother who brings ambivalence and complexity to Nesbit's storytelling. So far as the children – and Nesbit – are concerned, she is the ideal figure, beyond criticism. When Bobbie disobeys her by asking strangers for material or practical help, these are not shown as acts of rejection or defiance but difficult necessity and love. Mother is in several ways the opposite of the children. They make friends; she does not. They explore railway, station and village; she stays at home, or takes the train to a nearby town. They are indifferent to privacy; she sets great store by it. They ask for help; she forbids them to, and never does so herself. They are middle-class but indifferent to class boundaries; she chooses isolation rather than endanger their class status by exposing their beleaguered economic plight (and shameful family secret). They introduce people to the house (the Russian, the old gentleman, and Jim); Mother's privacy is breached only by compassion for the sick and injured. In a difficult passage in Chapter VII, even the old gentleman – after he has reunited the Russian prisoner with his family – is turned away, with impeccably polite discourtesy. Perhaps Mother fears for the secret of Father's imprisonment; perhaps she cannot bear that poverty should hamper middle-class obligations; either way, the episode prickles with class proprieties. And poverty is central to the problem.

But there are relativities in poverty. In Chapter I, when disaster strikes, Mother tells Bobbie, 'we've got to play at being Poor for a bit'. At first the play seems quite serious: bread and butter *or* jam; no fires in June; an inadequate invalid diet. But these extreme frugalities soon give way to gradations of poverty. After the truth of the old gentleman's hamper is revealed, and Mother's anger partly assuaged, she says, 'it's quite true that we're poor, but we have enough to live on'. There is poverty and middle-class poverty. Nowhere is this clearer than in Bobbie's conversation with the Doctor in Chapter IV, when medical expenses loom. Bobbie first repeats Mother's injunction that 'I wasn't to go telling everyone that we're poor'. And then, crucially, she says that Mrs Viney 'told me what a good doctor you were, and I asked her how she could afford you, because she's much poorer than we are. I've been in her house and I know'. Clearly therefore Mrs Viney is immensely poorer than the Doctor, yet Nesbit tells us, 'He was rather poor himself'. By what comparative standard?

Mrs Viney illuminates Nesbit's economy of poverty. In other books she might be numbered with the nameless. At the start, when it seems (wrongly) that she has not provided supper for the family's arrival at Three Chimneys, she is ' "a horrid old woman!" said Mother; "she's just walked off with the money" '. She makes regular small appearances throughout the book, doing menial tasks. Clearly Mother's poverty does not preclude at least one servant, and a loyal one. But at the end, when fortunes are changing in Chapter XIV and there are once again live-in servants, her hours are cut because the new staff tell Mother she is 'an old muddler'. Poor Mrs Viney; poor in two senses. Yet there is not the slightest sign that Nesbit feels the least discomfiture about her. Plainly Mother does not, and for practical purposes Nesbit *is* Mother, who is indeed a self-portrait.

So in matters of class and poverty the novel has an inconsistent ideology. The dominant voice is the children's – classless, outward-looking, generous in giving, asking and receiving. But it is 'placed' as one large act of innocent childness by their mother. She is authenticated in perfection by the author's approval, but is formidably middle-class within her boundaries of hard-pressed social custom. Both Mother and Perks abominate what they consider 'charity'. Their ethics of poverty are actually very similar, and admirable. They both value self-reliance, independence, reputation, pride, the autonomy of the family unit. But Nesbit cannot recognize them as virtually identical and equal. Mother's ethics of poverty constitute a moral virtue, a higher quality than Perks's estimable social pride. (And poverty in Russia is a separate matter; and poverty in Britain at the level of destitution and the workhouse goes unmentioned.) The overt ideology of the novel is actually the children's, but Mother, universally admired, is an ever-present alternative, tacitly endorsed by Nesbit. The author's active ideology of classless generosity and interchange is compromised by her passive ideology of material class difference.

iv) *Country and family: the politics of justice*
In terms of larger ideas and themes the pivotal chapter is clearly Chapter IV, 'Prisoners and Captives', and it may seem to bear out Peter Hunt's observation that Nesbit habitually 'sets up a potentially difficult situation and then withdraws from it'. The episode of the Russian Prisoner is the ideological key to the novel. On the one hand it is briefly subversive, introducing several bold ideas that are never followed through. On the other, it openly declares (through the unchallengeable voice of Mother) Nesbit's own most deeply felt priority, and also introduces (almost accidentally, it seems) the book's most radical and sustained departure from routine beliefs.

The Russian gentleman has suffered injustice, persecution, and the loss of his family in Russia, because he wrote a 'beautiful' book attacking tyranny and poverty in Russia under the Czars. The poverty of millions in Czarist Russia is a question of international politics, brought by the Russian prisoner to the children's domestic scene. Yet despite the obvious links, Nesbit makes no effort to connect it to the differential poverties of home, as considered in the previous section.

66

(The World's Classics edition of the novel, edited by Dennis Butts, is based on the sixth edition, published in 1944, which censored the text so that all references to Russian political cruelty were put in the past tense. This briefly makes a nonsense of the time-line, but was done because in 1944 Russia was Britain's wartime ally, ruled by a well-known humanitarian called Joseph Stalin. It is a warning of the danger in meddling with texts. However inconvenient it is, we need to re-enter the time when a work was written, and be extremely gingerly about updating it.)

Important as the theme of poverty is to Nesbit, the question of injustice is more so. Clearly the Russian has been indefensibly convicted and imprisoned for a crime against the state. So has Father, as Mother knows and all but the doziest readers have inferred, even if the children have not. Peter naïvely believes that there is no such thing as penal injustice; he is, after all, an English boy. Briefly, Mother questions the absolute in Peter's faith, and implies a connection with Father. Peter has said that 'people only go to prison when they've done wrong'.

'Or when the Judges *think* they've done wrong,' said Mother. 'Yes, that's so in England.'

Lightly and carelessly read, this is a patriotic defence of the homeland, where such injustices do not happen. In practice (with Father's fate in mind) it declares the fallibility of justice, even in England. This is bold writing. But Nesbit follows it up only with a single, inconspicuous word, at the very end, when passengers on the old gentleman's train are reading of Father's release 'and seemed very astonished and, [my italics] *mostly*, pleased.' This little adverb signifies the discomfiting truth that many people, then and now, are reluctant to accept the innocence of convicted people, because like Peter they cherish the dangerous myth of infallible justice, and feel threatened when it fails. Nesbit's whole plot depends on flawed justice, but her language scarcely admits it: ideology is almost buried under narrative.

There is a slightly different consequence of national injustice, however, which in Nesbit is more prominent. The Russian prisoner has escaped by volunteering as a soldier in wartime, and then deserting. Orthodox male Peter is troubled by this one, too.

> 'But that's very cowardly, isn't it' – said Peter – 'to desert? Especially when it's war.'
> 'Do you think [says Mother] he owed anything to a country that had done *that* to him? If he did, he owed more to his wife and children. He didn't know what had become of them.'

The question of cowardice is glossed over, it seems, though I shall argue that in the event it was not. It certainly cedes primacy to a division of loyalties, and the claims of family to be a higher loyalty than claims of country. The always reliable and humanitarian Bobbie, free of Peter's stock reactions, at once speaks up to reinforce Mother's priorities. Family comes first. And this (as we shall see conclusively later) is the dominant active ideology of the novel, emotionally outgunning the concurrent ideology of reciprocal altruism. Nesbit is at one with E.M. Forster's famous statement in his essay 'What I Believe': 'if I had to choose between betraying my country and betraying my friend, I hope I should have the guts to betray my country.' 'Such a choice,' said Forster in 1939, 'may scandalise the modern reader'. The emotional force and narrative tact of Nesbit's writing are such that it has not scandalized successive generations of *The Railway Children*'s readers. She gets away with it because its ideological centre of gravity is neatly transferred to Russia.

v) Male and female courage

Though Peter's conventional assumption that desertion in war is an act of cowardice is subordinated to the higher imperative of family love and loyalty, it seems to have opened up a new ideological pathway for Nesbit, which grows more and more important. Peter's question comes almost half way through the novel. Before it there has been mere passing reference to bravery. (On the last night in the old house, Bobbie sees Mother's face and murmurs to herself 'Oh, Mother ... how brave you are! ... Fancy being brave enough to laugh when you're feeling like *that*!') But after Peter's comment, bravery returns again and again in the narrative, with its own vocabulary: one negative –

cowardice – and four positives: bravery, courage, valour and pluck. In the next chapter after Peter's concern about Mr Szezcpansky's possible cowardice in war, the children themselves perform the first of their three acts of outright bravery when they witness the landslip and save the train. After this comes their reward: a presentation by the railway company. What inviting form will this take, they wonder. Typically, Bobbie has some compunction about the propriety of any award at all. Should they 'be satisfied with just having done it, and not ask for anything more?' Peter is in no doubt that more is appropriate, and again he thinks in military terms.

'Who did ask for anything more, silly?' said her brother. 'Victoria Cross soldiers don't *ask* for it; but they're glad enough to get it all the same. Perhaps it'll be medals.'

The Victoria Cross is the highest military award for bravery in Britain, and as Dennis Butts notes, it may have been in Nesbit's mind because in the recent Boer War (1899-1902), seventy-eight Victoria Crosses had been awarded. Peter's analogy is a grandiose one, of course, and there is plenty of humour in Nesbit's account of bravery's reward. But the chapter is titled 'For Valour'. 'For Valour' is the inscription on the Victoria Cross, and it is fair to assume that this is not just a tongue-in-cheek Nesbit joke. She is implying a direct comparison, however different in scale, between the bravery of soldiers and the bravery of young children. Acts of courage, she suggests, do not have a military patent but are within reach of anyone, even the very young. This is almost instantly reinforced in the next chapter, when the children rescue a baby from a burning barge. The text ennobles courage as a civilian and a childhood quality, and detaches it from military limits.

The disengagement of courage from war is taken further later. After the children have rescued Jim from the railway tunnel, and while Dr Forrest is setting Jim's broken leg upstairs at Three Chimneys, Peter teases the girls downstairs with gory images of suffering on 'the field of battle', ostensibly on the pretext of inducting Bobbie and Phyllis to their future as Red Cross nurses. (It is one of *The Railway Children's* accidental retrospective ironies that Peter is exactly in the age-group fated to be mown down only ten years later in the First World War, and Bobbie and Phyllis to carry out just those nursing duties that Peter scares them with, and worse.) Peter's heartless game of suffering (culled from his reading) earns reproof from Dr Forrest when he comes downstairs from setting Jim's leg. He contrasts their (actually Peter's) childish antics with the genuine suffering of Jim, whom he describes as a 'Plucky young chap'. Courage and pain in the world of military cliché are set against those in the everyday world, the lives of civilian man and boy. Nesbit is not unjust to Peter. Earlier he too has shown courage and fortitude when his foot was pierced by the garden rake, and in his painful recuperation has drawn strength from overhearing Bobbie's angry and fortuitous tribute, 'he's not a coward!'

More important still, Nesbit depicts and affirms the value of courage not only in civilian man and boy, but civilian woman and girl. Bravery is first deprived of status as a quality exclusive to militarism, and then to masculinity. In Chapter XII, when the children trace the injured Jim in the railway tunnel, Peter announces with pride to the sufferer that 'we are a rescue party', and gets the satisfying response, 'You've got some pluck, I will say'. This is to the family group. But things are different when Peter and Phyllis have gone for help and Bobbie is left alone in the dark tunnel with Jim. (Her bravery, coolness and practical nursing skills in this episode naturally highlight the injustice as well as the unfeeling childishness of Peter's subsequent taunts.) Jim, having first noticed that both girls' names can be abbreviated to boys', then says 'You're just as brave as a boy.' Of course she is, and poor Jim may sound condescending to a modern child reader, schooled in gender equality (though one suspects that gender principle is still ahead of practice). But in 1905 this is a forward-looking statement of enlightened principle on Jim's part, and in Nesbit's active ideology of courage, which we here see gathering momentum chapter by chapter, it raises the status of both children.

In case we have missed the point, Dr Forrest takes this further when he engineers a chance to talk to Peter after his reproof of Peter's heartless game. Some of this conversation in Chapter XIII may now seem dated, relying as it does on a very sharp and clear-cut gender division, though even this plainly derives from Nesbit's understanding (and hence Dr Forrest's) of what a boy of Peter's age already believes and can be expected to take. (The tacit and accepted and hence normative ideology of 1905 is now the unorthodox and jarring one, especially its biology of motherhood, although again there is a present-day difference between officially accepted gender norms and the actualities of underlying practice.) Dr Forrest starts by saying what Peter 'knows'.

> 'Boys and girls are only little men and women. And *we* are much harder and hardier than they are – ' (Peter liked the 'we'. Perhaps the Doctor had known he would.) – 'and much stronger, and things that hurt *them* don't hurt *us*.'

His explanation that this distinction is a biological necessity for the demands of motherhood will now raise hackles where it would not have in Nesbit's day. But what follows is the point of the whole conversation.

> 'They're awfully brave, you know ... Think of Bobbie waiting alone in the tunnel with that poor chap. It's an odd thing – the softer and more easily hurt a woman is the better she can screw herself up to do what *has* to be done. I've seen some brave women – your Mother's one,' he ended abruptly.

Nesbit can be seen here in the very act of moving the ideology of the children's book towards modernity. Unsurprisingly, she sounds one or two retrospective discords. But the main thrust of the narrative is indeed subversive and essentially – from a present-day perspective – enlightened. Not only does Nesbit demilitarize the property of courage, and free it of gender ownership, but in practice she extends its meaning. Courage for her is not solely the act of instant brave group leadership in emergencies (which is Peter's strength), but of solitary resolution and extended fortitude (which are Bobbie's, and also Mother's), and of brave practical empathy (which is Bobbie's own great gift). Thus residual gender differences remain, but only as the underlying springs of an equalized virtue. In this respect Nesbit writes as a feminist.

Finally she elevates courage to the highest of human attributes. Shortly after Dr Forrest's talk with Peter, Mother talks to him about their missing father and her belief (which Nesbit is honest enough to make her also *disbelieve*) that God will make everything come right.

Mother once again merges with Nesbit, author and character at one, for the conclusive affirmation: 'Courage, courage! That's the finest of all the virtues!'

vi) *The railway*

So far I have given various examples of *active* and *passive* ideology in Nesbit's novel, but have said nothing about the third category, *organic ideology*, where individual authorship and readership are influenced by the communal spirit of the age. In *The Railway Children* it is best exemplified by the book's most important character: the railway itself.

Historically Edwardian England was in some respects two simultaneous worlds. We think of it as a kind of golden age before the horrors of the First World War. England was at peace after the Boer War; the British Empire was at its zenith; the nation appeared prosperous and settled; the arts, ideas and politics were flourishing; and family life for the middle classes was based on stable values, giving pride of place to children and childhood, for whom it produced an outpouring of distinguished children's literature, of which *The Railway Children* is itself a part.

All this was actually a beautiful illusion. The reality of domestic politics included disturbing things for conservative households to contemplate: the rise of the Labour Party made left-wing attitudes not just a theatre of middle-class ideals but a force of active politics for the working class; the Liberal Party introduced the beginnings of the welfare state; the status of the House of Lords was challenged, as was the traditional balance of power between the sexes. There was political ferment as well as imperial confidence. And the international sky was darkening. In *The Railway Children* we hear of suffering people in Russia. Germany is never mentioned. But the First World War did not come out of the blue in 1914; the growing threat from Germany had caused alarm throughout the Edwardian decade. For the English middle class its family life was a domestic light surrounded by a gathering darkness. The double nature of the times formed the 'organic ideology' of the period, and in this novel we can see that double nature faithfully reflected in the railway.

In the immediate lives of the children the railway is an image of

72

settled domesticity. It is a centre of warmth and friendship. The children wave to the trains, and befriend the Station Master, the Porter, and a driver and fireman who can help to mend a toy engine. Although the railway tests them with serious local dangers – a landslide, a sleeping signalman, an injured boy in the tunnel – these if anything make the railway itself seem safer, because they strengthen the children's bond with those who run it. Peter's early misadventure with the coal is the shape of things to come. Despite the hardships, the children's life is secure and good. The railway is an extension of the family itself.

But the railway has a second character. At the beginning it transports the children into exile, and deposits them at night in a strange place. At the end it brings their father back from unjust imprisonment in his own country. In the meantime it has taken Mother off to periodic prison visits at an unknown place. It has brought to their own station platform a sick, weary and lost Russian gentleman, a refugee from cruelties beyond description. The railway is both the keystone of domestic happiness and a conveyance to and from a darkening world. The doubleness of the railway is the doubleness of Edwardian England, and Nesbit's book thus faithfully reflects the organic ideology of her age.

vii) *The ending*
The Railway Children has a happy ending: so much seems obvious. The broken family is made whole again by the return of Father. We watch the door close behind Bobbie and her father, and we go away, content that at last justice has been done, innocence vindicated, family love replenished and secure against the wider world's assaults – just as it was for the Russian prisoner earlier.

Things are back more or less where they started. In the opening pages, before Father's arrest, evening callers were assumed to be collectors for charity. 'Get rid of them quickly, dear,' said Mother, and Roberta wishes they had a moat and drawbridge so that 'no one could get in'. The watchword of the family unit is emotional (as well as material) self-sufficiency. Father and Mother are loving and attentive, and their focus is on family values. No one else is needed (except, of course, the servants). At the end we, the readers, are outside the closed door, left to imagine a resumption of happiness in which there is no place for us, even to look:

'we are not wanted there,' the author tells us. The ideology of family supremacy – Mother's ideology, and Nesbit's – is triumphant.

This only happens because that other strand of ideology – reciprocal altruism, trust, interchange of wider local kindness – is demoted. It is understandable that the distant, unseen, unheard but deeply felt political world of government in England and in Russia is shut out: its large impersonal injustices have caused great damage. And Jim, still mending his leg, is somewhere within, the wider world's one tolerated alien (apart, of course, from the servants). The old gentleman, his grandfather, can no doubt call, but we remember that even he was once politely turned away. And what of Perks, or the Station Master (but for whose kindness Peter might not be there)? What of all the friends the children have made by their openness? What of that outgoing, innocent, exploratory energy on the children's part, the energy that has recruited allies and, by proving that self-sufficiency is not enough, has enabled this ending to happen? All this, all these, like we ourselves, are outside the closed door.

There is an interesting small marker of social change at the end of the famous 1970 film adaptation of this book. In the film Mother is briefly glimpsed observing the approach of Father and Bobbie from behind the curtain. When they reach the house, Bobbie opens the door, Father goes in, and Bobbie closes it from the outside with a decided clunk. The children are on the outside, the others gathered up by Bobbie and taken away into the fields, while Father and Mother enjoy their reunion within. Bobbie uses Nesbit's words about herself and her readers – 'we are not wanted there' – about the children themselves, at least for a few minutes. This may be simply a narrative device to avoid the off-putting view of an empty field and a closed door, but it may also indicate a subtle change between Nesbit's ideology of the family and our own. For her it is a unified single organism, for us it is a unit, no matter how strong and interdependent, in which the adult partners are entitled to a greater insulation from their children. If so, it indicates a change in the organic ideology of modern family life.

I have shown, I hope, that *The Railway Children*, contrary to appearances, is not a simple text. (Although it is episodic, even its structure is not as simple as it seems: ideological advances are followed by events which reinforce them.) But at its heart the novel is a contest of two dominant ideologies – that of family self-sufficiency, and that of communal interdependent kindness: that of Mother, and that of the children. They are not mutually exclusive. Indeed, they embody a number of shared qualities and characteristics. But in her overall patterning and choice of ending, Nesbit does choose between them. All through the novel she has given increasing strength to the ideology represented by the children. But she reserves authority (in the full sense of the word) for Mother. In terms of ideology, the novel is indecisive and in some ways contradictory, but Nesbit in the end is not an impartial referee.

Two Ways of Reading

We are all familiar, in television dramas if not in person, with courts of law, and know the difference between judges on the one hand and counsel for defence or prosecution on the other. We know that their jobs are different. Lawyers acting for or against a prisoner are trying to persuade a jury to reach a particular verdict, whereas the judge is a kind of super-juror, seeking to act as an impartial, expert referee whose job is to weigh the evidence and help the amateur jurors to decide the truth. These roles have close equivalents in the work of teachers and critics who read fiction with or on behalf of children.

In the last two chapters I have tried to act as a judge. Although I cannot free myself completely of my own ideology, I have tried to do so with the aim of helping adult readers, and through them children, to interpret the ideology in other people's books – to listen and read carefully and form a view not only of what is said but what is thought and felt and hidden. I have been as objective as I can manage to be. In the next two chapters I exchange this role for that of advocate. Much criticism of all literature, including children's literature, is advocacy. The professional reader (counsel for the defence or prosecution) adopts an ideological standpoint which should be open and declared, though all too often it is not.

This standpoint may take many forms. At its most blatant we encountered it many years ago in Bob Dixon's two volumes under the title *Catching Them Young*, one subtitled *Sex, Race and Class in Children's Fiction* and the other *Political Ideas in Children's Fiction*. Dixon's own ideology is stridently declared, and he deals in simple terms with what I define as 'active ideology' in children's books. With much greater critical subtlety but similarly open commitment, Joseph Bristow's *Empire Boys* examines the fiction for boys published in the heyday of the British Empire. The book was generated by his own interests in imperialism, colonialism, masculinity and gender definition, interests which 'amounted to political obligations'. There is a wealth of commentary similarly produced from ideological standpoints, notably feminist criticism. These are perfectly reputable critical undertakings, provided they declare their interests and do not use the disguise of false impartiality to conceal political intent. Whether they are valuable or not then depends on the quality of their arguments and readings.

In the following two chapters I have put children's literature in the context of my own 'political obligations'. Ever since I was a schoolboy and became an amateur naturalist, my continuing concern has been the patently destructive impact of the human species on the planetary environment and its wondrous store of nonhuman life. Long ago it became apparent to me that humanity, which was endangering so much else, would finally endanger itself. The behaviour and environmental action of the human species have far outweighed for me alternative political concerns. Other people took the same view, though not enough to alter human behaviour in general.

I did not connect this side of my life with my work as a teacher of literature, and children's literature, until the 1980s, when I became aware of the strengthening current in new writing for children which in various ways reflected my own ideological position. The children themselves became newly significant, too, as it grew clear that damage caused by human beings would probably lead to crisis within one or two generations, much earlier than we used to think. I made connections, and the result is the following two chapters, which represent my own contribution to ideologically committed criticism.

Predicting catastrophe is an ancient and risky business. Dates for Armageddon foretold by numerous melancholy sages have arrived and gone, leaving the human race to go merrily on its way, unscathed. Dystopian fictions are not much damaged when their prophecies are discredited. No one thinks George Orwell's *Nineteen Eighty-Four* is obsolete because a less calamitous 1984 passed into history. Nonfictional predictions, such as lie behind the following two chapters, are more vulnerable to optimistic scorn, especially in retrospect.

It is instructive in 2011 to read *The Estate of Man*, by the poet and scientist Michael Roberts, posthumously published in 1951 and written in 1947-8. Roberts surveyed the material and social prospects for the human future, and took a sombre view of what he saw. He began by saying, 'There are 2,350 million people in the world, and the number is increasing at the rate of twenty million a year,' and he foresaw a major crisis if that population were substantially to increase. Now there are six billion of us, and the rate of expansion is far greater; but we are still here. Many of Roberts's predictions were based on projections which are plainly out of date, and it is easy to scoff at his whole searching enterprise. While much of the detail is long obsolete, however, it is alarming to see how much of his fundamental argument still stands, and has gathered ominous significance that he could not have foreseen. For example, his chapter on 'The World's Forests' now has totally different and more sinister resonances in the light of climate change.

There are risks in all such writing, and the viewpoint expressed in the following chapters, though not fictional, derives from the world of imagination, in which I work as a critic and teacher, rather than from science, where I have no claim to expertise. Even so, I invite anyone who prefers to dismiss these chapters as gloomily fanciful to read an important book by a major scientist, Sir Martin Rees, published in 2003. It is titled *Our Final Century*, and subtitled 'A Scientist's Warning: How Terror, Error, and Environmental Disaster Threaten Humankind's Future in This Century – On Earth and Beyond'. Rees is no alarmist visionary. Reason and science are his tools, not sombre futuristic dreams. He concludes in his final paragraph that 'humanity is more at risk than at any earlier phase in its history'.

As the reader will find in the following pages, I myself care more about life in general and less about humanity in particular than many other writers do. For those who do not share this bias, both Roberts's venerable analysis and Rees's recent one may still provide a sobering reminder that we live in interesting times.

The Darkening of the Green

Jonathon Porritt, then director of Friends of the Earth, has spoken positively about the 'light green' attitudes and actions that could be recommended to engage people's interest in defending their environment and to give them a feeling that they could make a worthwhile contribution of their own. There were changes in ideas and behaviour that could be adopted fairly painlessly, without undue disturbance to anyone's accustomed way of life. At the same time, Porritt acknowledged that there were members of the environmental and conservation movements who were privately committed to other, more radical views, involving an altogether darker shade of green.

In this chapter I shall recall some early and influential reading which had a decisive effect on my own beliefs, the colour of which is the very darkest green, shading into black. They will perhaps demonstrate what has been too often overlooked, that there is nothing new about 'green' attitudes. They will also illustrate the shaping power that children's literature can have, on individuals at least. On the basis of this personal experience, I shall try to explain why I find something missing, and something misdirected, in the most ideologically challenging literature for children being written at the present time.

Some of modern society's most committed environmentalists grew up during the 1940s and 1950s, the years of the Second World War and postwar recovery. Among the more obscure significances of those momentous years was the burgeoning effort to engage the interest of all children in the countryside and wildlife. Two individuals were particularly effective, and are held in affection to this day by those who heard their broadcasts on BBC *Children's Hour* and read the books that followed them. The pioneer was 'Romany' (Rev. G. Bramwell Evens), who conducted a long series of dramatized nature walks accompanied by his dog Raq and various 'learners'. The books evolved to match the format of the broadcasts and their enormous popularity with children. Early books such as *A Romany and Raq* show Romany chiefly in conversation with adult countrymen, but later ones, such as *Out with Romany by the Sea*, introduce the classic formula of adventurous expeditions shared by an adult and an eager, learning child. All the books were unashamedly 'faction' – their purpose was to teach natural history entertainingly and to communicate a sense of its value, and for that generation they succeeded triumphantly.

When Romany died in the late 1940s, his formula was inherited by a Cheshire naturalist, Norman Ellison, who assumed the deferential soubriquet of 'Nomad'. Ellison did not just follow in Romany's footsteps. He wandered further afield to more specific and spectacular locations, such as the underground caverns of the Derbyshire Peak District; and he invented some not very convincing brushes with danger. More importantly perhaps, he frequently introduced other books and authors (including Darwin's *Voyage of the 'Beagle'*) in ways that genuinely stimulated a keenness to read exploringly and a readiness to believe that reading was the doorway to exciting action, not only in books but in your own real life. Essentially, however, the didactic formula was the same as Romany's: a knowledgeable adult was teaching an interested child about natural history through the medium of imagined documentary encounter.

Although it is easy in retrospect to see naïveties in these books and broadcasts, they were at that time an achievement of remarkable originality and success. The formula was capable of much development, not least in the interplay of broadcasting and publishing. (Gerald Durrell's *My Family and Other Animals* belongs eccentrically to the same genus, and the book's magnificent title is not only a witty but an ideologically shrewd development of it.) Yet, disappointingly, the opportunities were not taken. Possibly children's tastes, but more probably the commercial and pedagogic steering of them, were diverted into other courses. Even television, which is beautifully placed to enhance such a formula, long neglected it. I can recall only one attractive but uneasy series, *Man and Boy*, which really tried to pick up the trail. The 'boy' of that series, Simon King, is now a producer of television wildlife films, and a presenter of the highly successful BBC

Springwatch and *Autumnwatch* programmes. The popular appeal of these live family broadcasts has done much to revive the dormant tradition after a long gap.

What these early books and broadcasts did was to show nonhuman life as having pleasure for ourselves and value in its own right. No radical views of human action are put forward; it is assumed that wild creatures have space enough to live their lives, and are there to be unobtrusively and undestructively observed by interested people. The underlying assumptions which really matter in them are that the stirring of informed enthusiasm must happen in childhood if at all, and that it must be both taught and caught.

I was permanently influenced by these books, as were thousands of others at that time. So I was by the first truly modern 'conservation' novel for children, Arthur Ransome's *Great Northern?* But alongside all these unteacherly teachers, there was another strand in the literature, potentially a more radical one. This is the Robinsonnade, the story that flows in direct descent from *Robinson Crusoe* and the adoption of that great mythopoeic novel into children's literature. Its most durable achievement from the postwar years (rightly described by Margery Fisher as 'this incomparable Robinsonnade') is 'BB''s *Brendon Chase*, the story of three superbly delinquent brothers who seize a golden chance to clear off to an unspoilt English forest and fend for themselves. The book has romantic wish-fulfilling excitement and abundant humour and fun, but also a realistic sense of practicality and hardship. The terms of the boys' choice mean that they must accept their status as intelligent animals, competing with other animals for the privilege of survival, and the book's constant implicit doctrine is that they must respect and guard the forest environment on which their living depends.

Although *Brendon Chase* falls short of equalizing *Homo sapiens* with other creatures in status and preciousness (and although most Robinsonnades have the same limitation) it does significantly narrow the gap and thereby pose an imaginative challenge which has never been more urgent. The Hensman brothers in *Brendon Chase* may be superior animals, and highly efficient tool-making predators, but animals they are. They enjoy no immunity from that complex pattern of interdependence which is now familiar as ecology. This is the strength and urgent value of the Robinsonnade as a story form: it cannot but disclose the human being's animal status, and disturb the complacent illusion of exceptedness by which we mostly live.

In 1950 another Robinsonnade was published for children, but unlike *Brendon Chase* it has not lived on into reprints and television adaptation. Today it is almost totally forgotten. The book is *Silver Flame* by Kenneth Allsop, who later became famous as a television presenter. I read about it in *Boy's Own Paper* when I was fourteen, and bought it. In ways that no doubt went far beyond its author's intention, it probably had a greater effect on me than any other book I read as a child or teenager.

Silver Flame is not an outstanding novel, and does not have the human comedy or variety of incident that set *Brendon Chase* apart. The story is very simple. Timothy, its thirteen-year-old hero, is interested in wildlife (and alas he collects birds' eggs, which was normal practice in 1950 but nowadays is fortunately not only illegal but unfashionable: some things actually improve). Near his home in the south of England is a zoo, something like a small Whipsnade. To this zoo are brought a pair of snow leopards. Timothy becomes infatuated with these animals, and more especially with the cubs they eventually produce. With the keeper to befriend and guide him (another knowledgeable mentor/boy relationship) he helps to rear them, and when their cage is destroyed in a landslide following a cloudburst, Timothy is at hand to rescue the one survivor. In secret possession of the cub, he plots to keep it. A few miles away is a large area of empty and forbidden Ministry of Defence land, the Battle Area, no longer used for training but closed to the public and abandoned to the wild. To this receptive wilderness Timothy and his friend John make their escape with the infant snow leopard, which they have called Silver Flame, and there for a year they live off the land. Their idyll of victorious hardship and privation ends when Silver Flame, grown to maturity, asserts his own true nature and leaves the safety of the Battle Area to kill sheep.

The book is not mainly about the snow leopard. Once the escape has happened he becomes largely peripheral to the story; revealingly, the author seems indifferent to him while he is a dependent pet, however exotic, and to become imaginatively engaged again only when the animal asserts its adult independent nature so bloodily. The boy protagonists are more interesting, but their characters are drawn in simple terms, and the strongest dramatic emphasis is on their mergence with the wild, their capacity to adapt to a new, primitive and self-reliant way of life, their absorption as rare predators into the intricate network of life-forms in the accidental wilderness.

Just occasionally in this 1950 novel a note of 'green' didacticism is sounded. When the boys come across a polluted stream, Allsop describes in detail the chain of chemical and biological devastation leading from a source in upstream factory effluent to the destruction of all fish and aquatic life. He comments:

> The poisoned stream was expression of the city's neglect of, and contempt for, the countryside; which is like a man, who has only one field on which to grow his food, digging it up because there is gold in the soil. He may become wealthy; but in the end it will mean death.

The book's thin scatter of such passages is significant: they show the ease with which the Robinsonnade crosses the border into parable. Elsewhere in the novel there is much digression into factual teaching about the creatures the boys encounter. The authorial voice adopts a tone quite similar to that of *Romany* or *Nomad*, and fiction becomes very close to faction. Yet the dominant impression of the book, its true imaginative achievement, lies in the powerful evocation of simultaneous life. In the Battle Area numerous diverse creatures live out their separate and yet intertwined existences.

As well as teaching about them, Allsop presents a series of perspectives of the world as it appears to nonhuman creatures. This approach is always open to the charge of anthropomorphism, but the strong imaginative empathy is accompanied by emotional restraint, and by conspicuous delight in the otherness of other creatures, so that this pitfall is skilfully avoided. The boys in their turn are not superior intrusive presences, representative of a different kind or order of being, but animals themselves and therefore part of the pattern. Their appeal and convincingness as characters lie precisely in that mergence, in their role as natural occupants of the life-filled habitat and not as alien controllers of it. Through their precarious existence the book presents a vision of the world in microcosm, the world as it might be, and realistically celebrates it.

In the pattern of postwar children's reading, the special place of *Silver Flame* is that it carries further, doctrinally and imaginatively, a kind of perception that could be seen in the documentary fiction of *Romany* and *Nomad*, in the early conservation novel, and in the other Robinsonnades such as *Brendon Chase*. Its classical precedents probably lie in stories about feral children, most notably the Mowgli stories of Kipling's *Jungle Book*. The imaginative power of *Silver Flame* (evident in muted forms in the other books) is that it is not a homocentric novel. It declares the separateness of other life-forms, makes implicit assertions of equal value in their shared life, accepts the animal identity of all creatures, man included, and settles unsentimentally for the presence of man the hunter while refusing to treat the natural world as an inferior order made for man's convenience.

In these respects *Silver Flame* went beyond the needs and orthodox understanding of its time – but not, as I shall argue, of ours. Kenneth Allsop had a singular gift for rendering through imagination as well as scientific fact the marvel of simultaneous life and the revolutionary change of perspective that ensues when you escape from homocentric thinking. He did it elsewhere in a memorable (but unremembered) volume of short stories about birds and animals, published for adults and revealingly entitled *The Sun Himself Must Die*, and years later in a superb television documentary on the wildlife of New York City.

Most human thinking is homocentric, naturally enough. Some centuries ago we reluctantly surrendered the idea of our own planet as the centre of the physical universe, but we still habitually think of our own species as the centre of organic life. It is always hard for people to stand outside their personal centres. Recent decades have shown how hard it is for members of one race to think multiracially, or of one culture to think multiculturally. For one species to think 'multispecially' is harder still. But failures in any of these respects are now a threat to our very survival, and failure in this third and hardest task is the greatest threat of all.

Like many teenagers I kept careful diaries and notebooks, so I can still retrace the steps of my adolescent thinking. The result is at the very least a testament to the importance of teenage reading and the effect that a single book can have. In *Silver Flame* I found a new way of looking at the world, one that was not homocentric, and the effect was liberating and inspiring. It would not have had the effect it did if *Romany* and *Nomad*, Arthur Ransome and 'BB', had not preceded it. And it could not have stood alone. Over the following two or three years I found other writers, and other perspectives, which had their share in forming my personal scenario for humanity. But *Silver Flame* was the indispensable link, the mid-river stepping stone but for which I would have been, for better or worse, a different person.

With some translation for brevity's sake into terms that were not then available to me, this is the view I came to as a teenager.

Over the last ten thousand years (a tiny fraction of our planet's life so far) the human species has enjoyed – if that is the word – an unprecedented biological explosion, generating ever-increasing populations, colonizing every type of habitat, using up resources in a species-time which is hopelessly unsynchronized with earth-time, causing short-term havoc in a world system which had previously experienced such alterations only in response to the slow hugeness of climatic or geological change. Although we might have enjoyed this explosion, for certain nothing else had. Viewed from the perspective of almost every other life-form on the planet, our epidemic spread during ten thousand years could only be regarded as a hideous infestation of powerful and destructive predators.

This biological success reflected formidable qualities: intelligence, rationality, adaptability, tool-making capacity, social organization, and much more. Even at fourteen one could not deny that these qualities included many attractive ones, above all the capacity for love, and also courage, imagination, artistic creativity, much else. Yet the balance sheet was clear. There were other animal characteristics all too evident in it: predation, greed, rapacious short-term opportunism, manic and irrational competitiveness. There were aggressive instincts fatally confused between the egotistical and the tribalistic. Whatever the achievements of the species, they were no counterweight to a dominant behavioural pattern which was destructive of other life, self-destructive, and patently unsustainable beyond the trivial time scale of a few millennia or even centuries. Despite the efforts represented by various moralities, and sanctioned by the invention of numerous humanoid gods, human intelligence was utterly incapable of controlling a suicidal pattern of animal behaviour. The Second World War was only just over, and unlearned lessons were everywhere to see.

Once started on the way, there was no difficulty in finding other challenging and confirmatory texts. As I have said, there is nothing new about 'dark green' thinking: it was alive and well in 1950, once you started looking. Here for example is Aldo Leopold, in the Foreword to his classic *A Sand County Almanac*, in 1948:

> We abuse land because we regard it as a commodity belonging to us. When we see land as a community to which we belong, we may begin to use it with love and respect . . . this much is crystal-clear: our bigger-and-better society is now like a hypochondriac, so obsessed with its own economic health as to have lost the capacity to remain healthy. The whole world is so greedy for more bathtubs that it has lost the stability necessary to build them, or even to turn off the tap.

Many years later I have found no good reason to revise the view I formed as a teenager. On the contrary, the intervening decades have supplied a steadily accumulating pile of evidence to confirm it. Recent opportunist political addictions to 'green' thinking collapse once they demand embarrassing and difficult choices. Their shallow expediency gives no sign at all that collective man, or collective woman, has changed its spots.

I am therefore left with a paradox or unresolved conflict between my private sense of worth and delight in human love and friendship and the everyday awareness of lives well lived, and my public sense of *Homo sapiens* as an over-successful and appallingly destructive pest species, incapable of using reason and intellect to reduce its numbers and change its behaviour, incapable of effective long-term thinking, and provably accelerating towards catastrophe, not in millennia or centuries but in decades. If this were just my conflict there would be little purpose in describing it, but it is not just mine; it is common to 'dark green' thinking everywhere. If its personal roots lay merely in the accidents of my own reading, there would be little purpose in linking it to children's literature; but children's literature in recent years has begun to generate many versions of the same conflict, and to outdistance adult novelists and social theorists in the radical nature of its visions. The heterodoxy of 1950 became the orthodoxy of 1990.

The conflict surfaces most memorably in perhaps the most outstanding children's book of modern times, Lucy M. Boston's *A Stranger at Green Knowe*, published in 1961, a decade after *Silver Flame*. *A Stranger at Green Knowe* is both a simple and a complex novel, in which the conflict of ideas about the human and the animal is artistically but not ideologically resolved. In its very compromises and uncertainties – which in no way disturb the formal coherence of the narrative – this story is a profound expression of the dilemma I am pointing to.

There are actually two strangers at Green Knowe in Lucy Boston's story. Green Knowe is an ancient manor house near Cambridge, guarded by its present elderly owner, Mrs Oldknow, who is the latest in a dynasty of owners stretching back to the early Middle Ages. Most of the stories about it are time fantasies, but this is the exception. One stranger is a refugee Asian boy called Ping, an orphan, who has spent some time at the house the previous summer (events recorded in *The River at Green Knowe*) and is invited back by Mrs Oldknow to give him a holiday from the hostel for displaced children where he usually lives. The other stranger is a young but fully grown gorilla, Hanno, a refugee from Regent's Park Zoo. Hanno is a displaced gorilla, captured in Africa and forcibly removed from his jungle homeland. Ping has already seen Hanno at the Zoo, and has become infatuated with him. Indignant at the animal's confinement, Ping is overjoyed when he escapes. By an absurd but wholly justified coincidence, Hanno finds temporary refuge in an undisturbed thicket at Green Knowe. There Ping discovers him, and there a brief, intense and tragic friendship grows between the two.

The complexity of *A Stranger at Green Knowe* lies in the fact that ideologically it both is and is not a homocentric novel. Part One of the book is a tour de force of non-homocentric writing, a marvellous act of imaginative empathy with Hanno in his jungle childhood. It renders with complete conviction the animal's feelings and behaviour, and those of his family group – especially his father and leader, the Old

Man – and his reactions first to the long luxurious freedom of existence in the tropical forest, and then to capture and confinement. The writing here and later is didactic in its indignation at human treatment of gorillas (its origins lay in Mrs Boston's encounter with Guy the gorilla at the London Zoo) and the lack of space for their independent existence caused by human actions and encroachment. The book is unquestionably a 'dark green' novel in a number of respects. It expresses delight and wonderment at this other, nonhuman, vivid life, and especially that brief part of it which is untouched by humanity. The separateness and the simultaneity of gorilla life are celebrated with great power.

Alongside this, the book is implicitly angry and despairing about human numbers. Whenever crowds of people appear in the story, they are treated with hostility and scorn, and contrasted with the secrecy and spaciousness of the gorilla's world. The comparative judgement is quite clear in the zoo scene, where the author records Ping's own rapt wonder and its interruption:

> . . . somewhere there was a country of such size, power and mystery that gorillas were a sample of what it produced in secret, where everything else would be on the same scale. The world always had surprises, and between every surprise there were other surprises. There was no end to what might be. Something like this Ping felt without words, losing all sense of time, while people of all kinds drifted past the cages.
>
> 'That's an ugly great brute to meet in the dark,' they said. They said it one after the other in procession, each as if it were an original remark. Only the tiniest children looked at Hanno without prejudice, and an infant in arms said 'Dad-dad' amid shrieks of laughter. Ping stood his ground while crowds formed and melted away.
>
> 'Coo! Aint 'e awful.'
>
> 'Oh look, darling, a gorilla. Isn't he a horrid big thing?'

The ideological content of this passage (all of which is repeated and writ large in the novel as a whole) repays close attention. It contains the following narrative signals:

– the large and hidden world is a place of mystery and rich potential, whereas confined and crowded spaces are trivializing and demeaning;

– the separate, sensitive and imaginative individual has access to intelligent vision beyond himself, whereas the crowd, and individuals conditioned by the crowd, are stupidly offended by strangeness: individuals diversify, but crowds standardize, both themselves and what they meet;

– the conveyor-belt stupidity of collective humankind is not connected with social class, as the last two comments neatly emphasize;

– children are more open, and more essentially intelligent, than adults are;

– confronted by a gorilla, adults observe repugnant difference (and teach it to their children) whereas children see delightful similarity.

These are all recurrent themes, and the last of them is particularly interesting as an indicator of the novel's artistic unity and ideological dividedness. But the rest deserve some comment first. For Mrs Boston humanity in the mass, in crowds (or even individually when purporting to speak for officialdom or collective attitudes), is profoundly different from the human individual occupying a private and secluded space (which may be, as for Ping in this episode, simply his own autonomous imagination). The difference is so great that it suggests two different animals, or different species. (And the difference is not a question of education or social class, though it is quite largely a question of age.) This intuition accords with the difference I noted earlier, between a coldly factual estimate of humanity's total biological performance and the warmer, localized reality of people's everyday affinities with their kind.

Lucy Boston is eager both to affirm the animal status of humanity and to adopt the long evolutionary perspectives within which the brief human explosion must be placed. She says of Ping in the Green Knowe thicket:

It was not like the beginning of the world – the Garden of Eden would surely have been more luscious, with pineapples and grapes

– but perhaps like the end of the world when man has been and gone.

and more uncompromisingly, in the mouth of one of Mrs Oldknow's visitors:

... perhaps in the end, if we don't exterminate the gorillas before we exterminate ourselves, the gorilla will have his chance. He's one of the really great ones of the earth, and he's not specialized, he's versatile. It's the versatile who survive.

In such passages we can see the reaching temporal imagination which is a natural part of non-homocentric thinking. The straightforward animal connection is another part of it:

... Hanno existed, a creature with the strength of a bull, the agility of a spider, the pounce of a lion, the sensitivity of a horse and the dignity and grief of a man – too much to take in, all the animal creation in one ... (44)

... Ping could not get used to the way Hanno's arms were dual purpose, equally good for whatever he wanted. It gave him great advantages which Man had thrown away when he decided to become two-legged. (101)

... Hanno's eyes ... combined the directness of a lion's stare with the interchange of a man's. (160)

But alongside these equalizing perceptions – man included with the animals – there is a contrary imaginative movement:

'They don't know anything about gorillas, do you, love?'
'Yes,' [Ping] answered coldly and politely. 'I do. I saw Hanno in the Zoo. He's a kind of a man.' (118)

... what [Ping] saw most clearly was the bare black human chest, so human it must be supposed to have human feeling. (123)

90

The Keeper had said Hanno never forgot. Sometimes he opened his lips as if he was about to speak. If only he talked he would be a man. But it was just his being both man and animal that made him Hanno. (124)

Ideologically Lucy Boston is literally in two minds. She sees humanity as animal, to be named in the same breath as other species, but also as different from other animals. She sees the gorilla Hanno as a being to be celebrated for his separateness and uniqueness, for the noble autonomy of his kind, but also as an animal resembling man and all the more precious and moving because of that close kinship and physical likeness. She sees value in Hanno's invisible jungle life, but also in the relationship he can form with a human boy.

This might be called a narrative device, especially since the book is for children. Perhaps the gorilla is made human (and childlike) in order to give young readers a point of access and sympathy, so that they will understand its difference more easily. You make Hanno familiar in order to make him strange. (This is a commonplace but self-defeating tactic in much sentimental, anthropomorphic writing.) However, Lucy Boston is not a writer who favours such compromises.

I think we meet a real and unresolved ideological division in the author. She admires Hanno in two competing ways: for his different-ness, and hence for qualities specific to gorillas, but also for similarity, for behavioural ideals which have human equivalents and invite a humanized descriptive vocabulary. This matter is complicated by the fact that in some respects the individual gorilla excels the corporate human. As this point will suggest, Lucy Boston also views humanity in two competing ways, expressed through the difference between Ping and Mrs Oldknow on one side and officialdom or crowds on the other. (Hanno's keeper occupies a midway position, and is a partly self-contradictory figure in consequence.) The difference is not simply between individual (good) and crowd (bad), and it is not fitted into the usual device of moral self-reassurance which people employ (we know we are imperfect, but single virtuous examples show us how good we can be when we try, so we may all improve one day; but not quite yet). The difference, as I have suggested, is more radical. As Lucy Boston presents it, humanity is two species at once, broadly split

91

between a noble individual and a degraded herd. Neither the gorilla nor the human being in *A Stranger at Green Knowe* is the focus of a single and consistent vision.

Artistically, the book is undamaged by these ideological fractures because of a brilliant narrative design and because there are two overriding simplicities of great power. Both Hanno and Ping are essentially ambiguous figures: this is precisely their imaginative attraction for the author. Hanno is the most humanlike of nonhuman creatures, while Ping is humanly admirable (polite, considerate, peaceable) but also a young animal, physically agile and graceful, and fond of solitary play. At the point when Hanno is shot, he is gorilla wholly (defending his adopted cub, Ping) and gorilla humanized (aggressively loyal to his loved kindred, a boy); Ping is human being wholly (of the ideal kind, compared with the gawping crowds of onlookers) and human animal (in momentary biological unison with the gorilla).

Both the double perspectives swim into single focus at the instant of Hanno's death. And overridingly there are an image and a moral principle. The image is child: Hanno, though 'adult' and 'parental', is still a young gorilla, near Ping's age; Ping stands for a possible evolution, a crucially different model for human futurity – not just in the way he behaves, but far more deeply in what he is. The moral principle is non-intrusiveness, reticence, respect for the biological space of other creatures (including people). This is violated at the start in the invasion of Hanno's jungle; it is institutionally violated by the Zoo; and it is violated at the end in the invasion of Green Knowe. Noninvasiveness becomes a unifying moral positive, the sine qua non of civilized individualism.

A Stranger at Green Knowe may be the greatest of all modern children's books. I think it is, but that is a matter of individual judgement. I am quite certain, however, that in retrospect it will prove the most important – the book, in Philip Larkin's phrase, 'in whose blent air all our compulsions meet'. It articulates more movingly than any book I know the paradox of humanity that we must learn to understand and live by if we are to survive at all.

For the present time the phrase I wish to stress, implicit as it is in all the foregoing argument, is 'two ways of looking at humanity'. At the outset I referred to a misdirected literature (though it is a powerful and distinguished one) and a missing literature. As to the first of these, consider the following roll call: *Children of the Dust*; *Brother in the Land*; *The Last Children of Schevenborn*; *Children of Morrow*; *The Sword of the Spirits*; *The Guardians*; *Empty World*; *Ransome Revisited*; *The Travelling Man*; *The Ennead*; *Divide and Rule*; *The Vandal*; *Z for Zachariah*; *The Timekeeper Trilogy*; *Return to the Gate*; *Futuretrack 5*; *Urn Burial*; *Devil on My Back*; *Plague 99*; *I am the Cheese*; *Torch* . . .

As these books go out of print and in many cases are forgotten, they are regularly replaced by new ones. This imaginative stream does not run dry. It is a sample of post-holocaust scenarios, explorations down the low roads of technology, cautionary political fantasies, metaphors for social and religious tyranny, and other nightmares which come within reach if we follow the blatant rationales of our own world to quite credible literal or metaphoric ends. There is a steadily expanding literature for children, more particularly for teenagers, which is bleakly pessimistic about the future of our planet. A recurring feature of it is the contrast between a few rebellious individuals (often children) and a repressive, rigidly unified, invasive, intolerant, hyper-conformist body politic, whether ultra-technological or (after the holocaust) neo-primitive in nature. Of course this contrast is a natural one for basic storytelling, but it goes beyond the ordinary limits of convention.

In many of these books we find the same essential difference that I have been tracing: not differences of behaviour and social structure within a species, but differences so radical that they suggest two separate species, or a choice of evolutionary outcomes. (This theme is brilliantly exemplified by John Wyndham's classic science fiction novel, *The Chrysalids*, published for adults but widely read by teenagers.) In contrast with the social theorists, who supply adult readers with numerous anodyne scenarios for the future, writers for children are increasingly depicting a world where there are few and spartan happy endings to be had. The best that can be offered in many cases is solitary or small-group survival in remote and uninvaded places – Robinsonnades of a dark future.

The centrepiece of most such novels, uncompromisingly excellent as they often are, is political or technological. Without seeking to undervalue this grim literature, or imply that its bleakness is gratuitous and unnecessary, I would still suggest that the weight of emphasis in our total futuristic literature is wrong. Underlying this literature are two intuitions, of particular significance for a teenage readership: that humanity will change, for better or worse, no matter what; and that humanity must change, or become extinct before its time. These are questions of biological imagination, but this kind of energy (so powerfully exemplified in Lucy Boston) is usually hidden beneath the immediate but more superficial lures of political and technological imagination. The ideological content of this fiction is typically very clear and openly declared, and its 'message' tends to be that humanity is dangerously at the mercy of its own political or technological artefacts. Underlying this explicit content is a half-conscious realization that these outward perils are traceable in turn to humankind's divided nature and potential. This division is characteristically expressed in terms of the individual at odds with the tribal, the outsider at odds with the conformists, the heretic at odds with totalitarian belief, and the child at odds with the adult. The last of these is often both symptom and symbol of disorder, because the child becomes the image of potential change.

In short, at deeper imaginative levels the drama occurring in these books is one of biological debate and confrontation, not merely a question of social, political or scientific behaviour. The imaginative responses to our own world which were already astir in 1950, enough for me to pick them up in my own teenage reading, are turning into a literature. And it is a timely one for a world in danger.

There is no profit in making silly claims for children's literature. It is not read as widely as we could wish, and still less is it taught in schools at the level of ideas and ideology. Children's books are not going to change the world, or perform any rescue acts. But they can help some children to think radically about their own species and the global habitat it should but does not care for, and that is well worth doing. After all, theirs may be the final human generation to have the chance. Even if a few of today's teenagers experiment with non-homocentric thinking, even if a few teachers are convinced of its value and learn to show them how, that is better than nothing. We have to do what we can. And it is worth remembering that just occasionally an individual story takes on a quality of fable and of myth, and so becomes a navigation light for the imagination and understanding of a much vaster audience. *Robinson Crusoe* did that. So did *The Jungle Book*. In modern times *Lord of the Flies* has rightly achieved the same status (Golding's boys stand for modern humankind when they set fire to the island on which their survival depends). A much older myth, and yet the most relevant and potent one of all for our present times, is Noah's Ark. We have the makings of a literature that just might produce another. But in order to supply what is currently missing in our story life for children, we need in more senses than one to go back to nature.

Holocaust literature, though often intelligent and disturbing, is ironically too starkly apocalyptic in its characteristic events and settings to stand unsupported as a literature of warning. Because it traces catastrophe to massive political and technological causes, it has two disadvantages. First, it suggests that the causes are institutional, and can therefore be controlled and corrected by human agencies at any time before the holocaust occurs. Conversely, it implies that we as individuals are helpless, precisely because the forces are so large. We cannot prevent; we can only survive. Individual human nature cannot grapple with collective human nature.

We are all aware of a possible Armageddon, but cannot let that displace the more immediate realities of disaster. Environmental calamity is made up of a myriad small events, not one climactic huge one, and it is happening now, not in some hypothetical future.

You do not need a world stage as the setting for a myth. Those I have cited managed quite well with an island, a patch of jungle, or a boat. I should like to see a scaled-down, touchable literature of the almost here-and-now, in which the commonplace predations of humankind, the ones familiar to us, are seen to confront the life of the natural world and force us to choose: we can have nature, or our present human nature, but not both.

These commonplace predations are very close to home. They happen all around us, every day. As we choose between nature and human nature in daily events, our numerous small choices are gradually building up to a global decision, composed from all these little ones, which is a decision to have neither. If we transpose the former competing theories of the origin of the universe to the threatened death of our planet, the outcome is more likely to be Continuous Destruction than a Big Bang. Stories of future catastrophe are important because they depict the longterm logical outcomes of our human behaviour, but we also need stories with events and settings which are inches from the everyday, and near enough to shock. They might compel us, rather better than apocalyptic fictions do, to recognize the choices and our own complicity in choosing. And they might help children to form that habit from the start.

Although much of the emerging literature is pessimistic, and although a 'dark green' literature cannot but pass a hostile verdict on the collective human performance of recent times, there is often a quite different and more challenging attitude involved in its presentation to children. Otherwise, why write it? Not to make children miserable, surely. Paradoxically, a literature of warning is written out of hope. Somewhere behind the authorial voices are the words of Mr Panwallah, the watchmender, to the boy Hari in Anita Desai's *The Village by the Sea*:

> Learn, learn, learn – so that you can grow and change. Things change all the time, boy – nothing remains the same. When our earth was covered with water, all creatures lived in it and swam. When the water subsided and land appeared, the sea creatures crawled out and learnt to breathe and walk on land. When plants grew into trees, they learned to climb them. When there were not enough plants left to eat, they learnt to hunt and kill for food. Don't think that is how things have remained. No, boy, they are still changing – they will go on changing – and if you want to survive, you will have to change too. The wheel turns and turns and turns: it never stops and stands still . . . You are lucky . . . You are young. You can change and learn and grow. Old people can't, but you can. I know you will.

The confident certainty of that last sentence is not echoed by some major writers of futuristic fiction for children. Nor could it be by those who present to children the history of the human animal's performance on this planet. We are tenants behaving like owners; joint tenants behaving like sole occupants; occupants behaving as if we had no inheritor. A latter-day Romany or Nomad could not now write as he did in the middle of the twentieth century. For my own part, I can see no grounds at all for certainty. But the hope is another matter; there is still hope. If all the children learn.

Hope Against Hope

'The Darkening of the Green' was first published twenty years ago. Returning to it in the light of what has happened since, I find almost nothing I would wish to change except perhaps the ending, which deals too superficially with the problem of hope. Hope, and its sibling optimism, are the focus of this afterword.

In 1990 'The Darkening of the Green' was a notably pessimistic essay, echoing and endorsing the attitudes expressed or implicit in much of the literature I dealt with. Pessimism does not readily win friends, especially as many people wrongly equate it with despair. Optimism and hope are widely regarded as moral virtues, not as attitudes of mind that may or may not be justified. They are even considered especially praiseworthy when they irrationally defy realities. To say 'I'm an optimist' is to win approval. In some circumstances the approval is probably warranted: an optimistic outlook seems to be genuinely helpful in recovery from illness, for example. But if optimism is considered an unconditional virtue, it naturally follows that pessimism is treated as a vice.

These words are often used as if they were absolutes. Yet they are almost meaningless except in contexts. To be comprehensively an optimist or pessimist is to be idiotic. 'The Darkening of the Green' expresses a deeply pessimistic view of collective humankind (but not of individuals), and of human impact on our fragile planet and its precious cargo of nonhuman life-forms. I also take a pessimistic view of humanity's survival prospects unless its numbers are reduced and its behaviour changed, and contemplate (with equanimity) a world in which humanity is extinct but other life goes on. How might an optimist respond? Here is a selection of imagined optimistic rebuttals:

I am an optimist. The picture you paint is unpleasant so it must be wrong.

I am an optimist. I know we are using up the world's resources at unsustainable rates, and causing climate change, and causing many creatures to become extinct, and generally creating mayhem on the planet, but so far I have suffered no personal ill-effects, and I think something will turn up to save us before I do.

I am an optimist. I believe that human ingenuity will provide new answers to humanity's needs, and humans have no responsibility to bother about anything apart from human interests.

I am an optimist. I think the world and everything in it was created by God for humans to enjoy, and God will take care of us.

I am an optimist. I believe I can go on greedily exploiting the planet for my own (or corporate, or national) advantage and profit for quite some time yet, and I'll be safely dead before Nature sends in the bill.

I am an optimist. I think that no matter how much damage we do, the planet will repair itself and life will continue or resume long after we are extinct.

As the reader will notice, the last of these is not exactly a rebuttal. On the contrary, it is the view I hold myself. And lo!, I am an optimist. But being an optimist in this longterm sense is not inconsistent with profound regret at the probable loss of all that is intelligent, creative and beautiful in humanity itself, or all that is precious in the multitudinous life-forms simultaneous with ourselves. So when someone says, 'I'm an optimist', I wish to ask, 'What are you optimistic about?' If someone says, 'There is hope', I wish to ask, 'What do you hope *for*?'

From very important matters like the survival of organic life, to very small matters like the evolution of fictions and their ideologies, it is important to go against the human grain and respect pessimism. We must outgrow the tendency to treat optimism and pessimism as virtue and vice, and instead ask for the evidence which in particular cases justifies (or fails to justify) one or the other.

A useful distinction can be drawn between what is thinkable and what is imaginable. What is thinkable is the province of politicians and of corporate opinion-formers, and I shall return to it. What is imaginable is the province of writers and artists and makers of fictions, and of their audience. The difference between the two is more evident and starker now than it was two decades ago, and brings in its wake more visibly than ever the problem of hope.

At the close of 'The Darkening of the Green' I found a place, however guardedly, for hope, especially in works designed for children. This view, I think, reflected general attitudes in 1990, and is beautifully exemplified in Robert O'Brien's 1975 novel, *Z for Zachariah*.

In O'Brien's post-holocaust scientific fantasy, atomic war has destroyed the world except for one small fertile valley which is protected by a microclimate. Ann Burden, a teenager, survives there alone, apparently the last human being left alive. All life outside her miraculous enclave seems to be extinct. Then another survivor, a man in a protective suit, turns up to invade her lonely peace. Mr Loomis's arrival is not, as the relief of loneliness should be, good news, and after an increasingly hostile relationship reaches crisis point, Ann is obliged in desperation to steal his safe-suit and flee her valley. She has no idea whether any other protected microclimates and groups of survivors exist elsewhere. She may be exchanging Loomis and her valley for a poisoned and unpeopled wilderness. But at the end she is given a shred of hope, as Loomis shouts from his stolen valley that in the west, before his arrival, he saw birds flying. Ann leaves, searching the horizon, and her last words are 'I am hopeful'.

Already in the many dystopias for children up to 1990 hope was a severely rationed commodity, and a bleaker pessimism was reshaping the imaginable, even for children. In 1988 Peter Dickinson's *Eva* was published. This extraordinary novel has proved lastingly popular and influential. In 2008 it won the Children's Literature Association Phoenix Award for a title 'which has maintained reader satisfaction for 20 years'. The teenage readers who find *Eva* satisfying clearly live in a changing world of imaginative expectations, because such hope as *Eva* offers is not hope for humankind.

The novel's imagined future is one in which a hugely expanded human over-population has destroyed virtually all other life-forms. Nonhuman life is all but extinct. It survives in the old wildlife films watched by people on the 'shapers', or futuristic television screens, in their apartments. Such technological entertainments in small private cells of existence take up much of people's lives. Ruthless corporate interests control society, such as it is, and subsidize the work of scientists like Eva's father, who is in charge of a collection of captive chimpanzees. This small pool of animals is kept for public entertainment, advertising gimmicks, and biological research. At fourteen Eva, an attractive girl, is the beneficiary of this research when an accident leaves her ruined body in an irreversible coma. To save what can be saved of Eva, her 'neurone memory' is transplanted into the body of a chimpanzee. Her mind and memory and personality are intact, engaged in delicate experimental negotiation with the body and physical life of humanity's closest animal relative. As Eva progressively identifies herself, or much of herself, with the chimpanzees, and fights successfully for an island refuge in which a chimpanzee society in miniature can live independently of humans, so human life itself begins to collapse under the weight of its own numbers and gradually loses the will to live.

The whole of this 1988 novel is a verdict on the human performance consistent with the one presented in 'The Darkening of the Green'. Its essentials are the same: an indictment of human over-population, catastrophic impact on biodiversity, habitat destruction, together with appreciation that the process is self-limiting, that the human orgy of extinction must eventually include humanity itself. In a key passage one of Eva's human supporters, Grog Kennedy, sets out for her his view (and in ideological terms the novel's view) of where humanity stands in this logical continuum of present-day behaviour:

'Trouble with us humans is we keep forgetting we're animals. You know what happens when an animal population expands beyond what the set-up will bear? Nature finds ways of cutting them back. Usually it's plain starvation, but even when there's food to go round something gets triggered inside them. They stop breeding, or they eat their own babies or peck each other to death – there's all sorts of ways. Us too. It's in us. We can't escape it. A lot of it's been going on already for years without anyone noticing, a sort of retreat, a backing-out, nine-tenths of the world's population holed up in their apartments twenty-four hours a day watching the shaper. But it's starting to move now. I can feel it. There's a real crash coming...'

The book's continuing popularity and esteem, its lack of datedness, may lie in the fact that this discomfiting scenario is set in a futuristic dystopia and is therefore not immediately threatening, yet is also on another level credible and recognizable. Massive population increase is now an obvious global phenomenon, yet some societies are experiencing a fall in the birthrate and a shortage of children: ever-inflating global numbers coincide with demographic crises linked both to ethnic and cultural disparities and to the balance of age-groups within populations. Human numbers are now linked to consciousness of poverty and increasing fear of food shortages.

Later in the novel another character tells Eva (now on her island with her fellow chimpanzees) that human will is subsiding into inertia and even suicide, a condition seemingly very unlike our world, divided as it is between primitive fanatical zeal and apathy. But individual feelings of political indifference, of impotence and boredom, of nihilism, of being surplus to the world's requirements, are widespread and increasing. When *Eva* was written, and depicted people shut in their apartments watching shapers, the internet did not exist. Who in 1988 could have predicted a global society in which people in their tens of millions seal their lives inside a virtual world? Dickinson dared to offer his teenage readers a world almost devoid of hope, and he has kept his readers over two decades during which at least some of his disturbing visions have moved noticeably closer to perceived realities. Taken alongside other fictions in books and films which have appeared in the intervening years, this suggests that – almost without our noticing, perhaps – the imperative of hope has weakened.

In some respects *Eva* resembles Lucy Boston's *A Stranger at Green Knowe*, though in a more developed, complex, radical form appropriate for an older readership in darker times. Both books concern the relationship between humans and one of their closest animal relatives, gorilla or chimpanzee. In both stories the animal relative is endangered. In both it is caged and exploited, for human entertainment or convenience. In both the animal relative escapes, though briefly in Boston's story, to freedom in a sympathetic environment. In both there is a fundamental contrast between humanity in the mass and one individual (Ping, Eva) who attains some form of biological affinity with the nonhuman animal. And crucially both stories postulate a possible, however unlikely, distant future in which gorilla or chimpanzee will survive, in Boston's words, 'when man has been and gone'.

Neither story does more than glance in passing at this prospect. In the present world it is obviously at the distant edge of practical credibility, but it accords with the intuition in both novels of the course that humankind is taking and its likely end. In *Eva* the chimpanzees' post-human future is merely the vision of a fringe group of eccentrics whose 'idea is that chimps are the human future. They call you the Inheritors'. Thus, however discreetly, Dickinson introduces the idea, and reinforces it at the very end when the dying Eva, who has looked out from the island to 'the distant blue loom of Madagascar', thinks of chimpanzee descendants who might one day 'experiment with a raft'. What is important here is the imaginative engagement with a nonhuman future, and the sympathetic equanimity of its artistic voicing. It is an idea which is now becoming more familiar. And in this world the chimps will *not* be 'the human future'. *Eva* differs from *A Stranger at Green Knowe* in *not* recruiting the human element as part of the case for biological transmission. Ping in Boston's story said of the gorilla that 'He's a kind of a man'. Dickinson, by contrast, lays stress on the fact that although the chimps have learned from Eva skills that may be vital to their evolution, she has no genetic legacy: her body remains that of the chimpanzee in whom she was implanted. The boundary of the imaginable is being stretched.

The 'thinkable', if we define it as the province of the politicians and of those whose interests they serve, is another matter. It is undeniable that the twenty years since *Eva*, and since I wrote 'The Darkening of the Green', have brought unprecedented political attention to environmental matters. The reason can be summed up in two words: 'climate change'. Scientists were already concerned with climate problems before 1990, but only since then have they seized political and public attention, and only against constant sceptical attrition from those who find the potential results of climate change or its mitigation uncomfortable and (worse) inconvenient and (worst of all) expensive. The scientific evidence confirming climate change is (typically of our species) indisputable and disputed. It has become not only 'imaginable' (for writers of fictions) but 'thinkable' (for politicians). There have been extraordinary changes in the political culture over twenty years. Luckily, climate change is inseparable from the other two items in the unholy trinity of human mischief-making, erosion of biodiversity (and the extinction of species) and human over-population, so that the ideas I expressed on these two questions in 'The Darkening of the Green' now seem justifiably pessimistic and less controversial.

Unfortunately the 'thinkable' for politicians does not enjoy the freedoms of the 'imaginable' for artists. When Tony Blair became Prime Minister of Britain in 1997, he appointed Frank Field as a minister to 'think the unthinkable' on some questions of social welfare. A year later he dismissed him for doing exactly that. This small event encapsulates the record of the world's politicians during twenty years of mounting evidence of catastrophe. Human over-population is virtually a taboo subject across the political world. There is gestural talk of how to feed the increasing human billions, but not of how to reduce and reduce these numbers to sustainable levels. (There is certainly a need to 'think the unthinkable' here, but in practice we shall wait until Nature does it for us.) Biodiversity is no longer a marginal issue to be left to conservationists. It is accepted as a cause demanding political action. So there are more gestures. And are they effective? They are (I use the word deliberately) hopeless. *The Times* in London reported in October 2010:

> . . . the opening in Nagoya, Japan, of an important international meeting on the protection of wildlife. More than 190 countries will try to agree new targets for halting the loss of species, under the Convention on Biological Diversity.
>
> Britain, in common with every other country, has failed to achieve a target set in 2002 to reduce the rate of species loss by this year.

Two things must be underlined in this shameful record. First, the original aim was a very modest one: to reduce the *rate* of species loss, not species loss itself. Second, since the target has not been reached anywhere, and mere stability is implausible, this means that the rate of species loss has actually increased. Everywhere.

As for climate change itself, the science is on record, as are the efforts of multinational companies and other interested parties to discredit it. There are plenty of optimists. (See above.) For the political realities, we need only note the events at the Copenhagen Climate Change Conference in December 2009, where the 'thinkable' became too ambitious and collapsed in an embarrassing political fiasco. Alas, it was the diplomatic shambles and resulting annoyance of posturing national leaders that emerged as important, not the lost chance to ease planetary danger. A year later another conference tried to mend things, but only did so by settling on a form of words so untroubling to climate vandals that nothing of significance was achieved. Only one country out of all those present – Bolivia, to its everlasting credit – dissented from the 'thinkable' conference document, finding it to be inadequate. In any case, who seriously expects China or the United States, the chief offenders, to step off the primrose path to the earthly bonfire? Both countries are full of optimists.

As Tony Blair found out, the 'unthinkable' is risky terrain for politicians, leading straight to what George Orwell famously termed 'doublethink'. The political class internationally knows the facts and reliable scientific projections for the human future, and the planet's. It is unthinkable to endure the global consequences of climate change, but unthinkable to take the actions needed to reduce and slow it. It is unthinkable to allow a mass extinction (for quite selfish human reasons, as I shall shortly illustrate) but unthinkable to do what is needed to stop it. It is unthinkable to let human numbers exceed the planet's tolerance, but unthinkable to reduce them.

So what *is* thinkable? Statements of intent, targets, conferences, and inadequate gestural actions (such as wind farms) are thinkable. Resolute words are thinkable. How many times over the last twenty years, as some new alarming scientific evidence or global climate event has occurred, have we heard politicians say 'This is a wake-up call', and then reach for political sleeping pills? Political humankind now lives in a condition of neurotic optimism, medicated by the language of urgency and the action of deferral, and thus able to live (for now) quite literally 'in two minds'. There is now, in my view, no warrant at all for political hope.

So the 'imaginable' becomes steadily more important, for ourselves and our children. Sometimes even now there is a boundary to be drawn here. Although the contract between the makers of fictions for the young and their audience has found ever greater space for pessimism and abjured protective caution, there are still some visions 'for adults only', though it sometimes seems that adults are less resilient than teenagers. One such work is the novel *The Road*, by the great American novelist Cormac McCarthy. McCarthy is certainly not one of America's optimists. *The Road* is perhaps the finest and most extreme dystopian vision of all. In this novel all life, animal and vegetable, is dead, except for a small and dwindling remnant of human survivors. We do not know what has caused this ultimate disaster. The one brief flashback to its origin suggests perhaps an act of suicidal warfare, but more probably asteroid impact of the sort that destroyed the dinosaurs. Some years later a man and his young son are heading south through a burnt and lifeless America, in search of refuge from perpetual winter. Wherever in the desolation they encounter groups of humans, there is danger. The last few stores of canned food from the pre-disaster world can still be found, and there is water, but since everything else is dead the only fresh food for humans now consists of other humans. McCarthy therefore depicts a world entirely without hope. *The Road* is the ultimate and unsparing imaginative proof of humankind's dependence on biodiversity.

The only positive thing in McCarthy's bleak human finale is the love between father and son, a love which extends in the young boy to a generous if impotent compassion for anyone they meet in even worse case than themselves. They are, as the boy often wants to be reminded, 'the good guys'. There are very few left. At the end the father dies, having fought a sickness just long enough to put the boy in the path of another small family of 'good guys', who adopt him. It is a 'happy ending' only in the narrow sense of affirming the marginal survival of the best of humanity, human love. But it is only a provisional survival. It will only last until the food runs out. There is no other life at all.

The Road was made into a film, which is beautifully acted and in most respects astonishingly true to the novel. Alas, it does not quite keep its nerve. Towards the end, there is a glimpse of a living beetle, then (as it might be in *Z for Zachariah*) a glimpse of birds, and at the last, when the boy meets his adoptive family, they have a dog. These tiny details fatally compromise not only the utter hopelessness of McCarthy's vision but the centrepiece of his thought: the uninhabitable nature of a planet without other life-forms than the human. There is no place even among adult audiences, it seems, for a film entirely without hope.

The Road is perhaps a step too far in finality for children's and teenage literature to emulate it, but many dystopian novels for teenagers run it close. So it is worth emphasizing how even this darkest of visions retrieves an illusion of hope where it can. The species is doomed, but the novel is filled with longing for the boy to survive, at least to live his own life out as what he is, the best of humanity, the recipient and giver of human love. Even the implacable McCarthy therefore reflects the conundrum that runs through these two essays and the literature they explore: the ambiguity of humankind, expressed in McCarthy as in so many other fictions in the contrast between collective humanity and individuals.

So where does the 'imaginable' now find itself? Perhaps the most surprising development is the growing acceptance of a possible living planet without humankind. When this idea appeared fleetingly, but with approval rather than alarm, in Lucy Boston's *A Stranger at Green Knowe* (1961), it seemed eccentric. When it appeared in *Eva* (1988), it read as both disturbing and heartening, so skilfully did Dickinson adjust the balance of sympathies between humans and chimps. Certainly it was provocative. Two recent examples illustrate how it has largely ceased to be so. Here is a conversation in Julia Green's teenage novel *Drawing with Light* (2010), between sixth-former Emily and her boyfriend Seb:

> 'If something happened to all the human beings,' Seb says, 'in a very short time, England would be covered in trees again, like it used to be. One huge forest.'
> 'You say that as if it would be good,' I say.
> 'I like thinking about it,' Seb says. 'That we're not very

important, really. If we mess up the world, it will just recover. Nature will, I mean. There just won't be any people to see it.'

'So global warming and climate change doesn't matter?'

'Of course it matters! It will mean horrible things for millions of people. But the planet will adapt and recover. The earth will go on living.'

I think about that.

And it is plain that many intelligent teenagers now 'think about that', and are invited to do so in the present culture of what is imaginable. Even more remarkable is to find the same essential idea in a novel for younger readers, David Almond's *My Name is Mina* (2010) the prequel to *Skellig*. Mina, a middle-school girl who figured importantly in the earlier novel, here tells her own story and records the ideas thrown up from her solitary, intelligent and imaginative life. She has made a model of the archaeopteryx:

> And I think about how it was the dinosaur that survived the disaster that wiped out all the other dinosaurs. And it didn't just survive. It evolved and became more elegant and skilful and powerful. It started the line of evolution that led to birds! … And I've been thinking: if the human race manages to destroy itself, as it often seems to want to do, or if some great disaster comes, as it did for the dinosaurs, then the birds will still manage to survive. When our gardens and fields and farms and woods have turned wild, when the park at the end of Falconer Road has turned into a wilderness, when our cities are in ruins, the birds will go on flying and singing and making their nests and laying their eggs and raising their young.

One strand of the 'imaginable', in other words, is now the unhorrified contemplation of a living world without people, an idea that has quietly moved from what might once have seemed like misanthropy to the mainstream of conversation through story with children.

Naturally not all literature for children and teenagers is quite so content with a human-free future. Many versions of a manmade crisis are now in modern literature for both adults and the young, and they are far removed from the 'thinkable' irresponsibilities of political and commercial humankind. Their essence is beautifully expressed in a short story by Helen Simpson, 'The Boy and the Savage Star', published for adults but excellent reading for teenagers. Two second-year undergraduates, therefore twenty years old, are on a vacation cycling holiday in France. Having met at a summer term party, they are newly in love, experimenting joyously with mutual discovery and fresh relationship. The story is full of the personal hope that comes with youth, independence and sexual freedom. But they disagree about the future of the planet. Neither of them is an optimist. But Brendan, a geographer, is an environmental activist at university, and wants to recruit Adele to his group movement of protest and reform. Adele resists – not because she thinks his cause is wrong, but because she thinks it is already too late:

> He tried to make her promise to join him in his activism next term; it's no longer a case of crying wolf, he'd told her, the end of the world really is nigh. Too late, she had replied; it's too late. 'Money's won,' she'd shrugged. 'It's obvious.'

Their argument goes on, through the physical delight and intelligent adventure of their holiday, and creates a tension in their relationship – but by no means enough to spoil it:

> 'I'm not a gloom-and-doom merchant, Adele,' he wanted to say; 'you know I'm not; in fact, I'm a sight more of an optimist than you are.'
> He doesn't need to convince me, she thought. I know what he's saying. I just think it's hopeless and we're the last generation. The last but one, to be more accurate. Our children will be the last. That's my considered opinion as an historian, is it? Yes, it is.

Brendan in Simpson's admirable story denies being a gloom-and-doom merchant, though Adele, being more pessimistic than he is, is unlikely to have accused him of it. 'Gloom and doom', more usually 'doom and gloom', is an expression used by lazy-minded optimists to demonize pessimism, even when the pessimism is supported by evidence and argument. The term is a substitute for actual thought. But 'doom and gloom' is not a characteristic of environmental fictions, in the sense of being miserable and depressing. Societies have always explored serious, alarming, even apocalyptic themes through the medium of pleasurable images and narratives. (Consider Dante's *Inferno*, *The Pilgrim's Progress*, or Hieronymus Bosch's vision of Hell.) Environmental apocalypse is no exception. This is the great theme of our time, just as spiritual salvation and damnation formerly were. It is an immensely serious and important subject. And it generates wonderful stories.

Most people, most children, do not hear or read them. In spite of its urgent relevance to everyone, the future of human life on the planet is a minority concern. In general human beings are too busy with other activities, other hopes and fears, to take any notice. Most adults and children who do take notice nevertheless spend the bulk of their lives on other things, unparalysed by doom or gloom. Mina does. Emily and Seb do. Brendan and Adele do. Unlike the boy in *The Road*, or the children of other dystopias, we still have the happy option of multiple hopes, even those of us (like Adele) for whom longterm hope is dead.

Hope, for adults and children versed in the 'imaginable', is not an absolute but a spectrum. If we are lucky enough to live in rich countries and be free of the daily pressure to survive, we can rest everyday hope in the manifold pleasures and distractions of our proliferating electronic media and precarious consumer world. But when we diversify 'hope' beyond our immediate lives, it raises choices.

What do we hope for? Hope that the life of the world will go on without us? Hope that Nature will thwart our mischief before we have wiped out other life? Hope that even now it is not too late to do needful 'unthinkable' things? Hope that the children of today's teenagers and students will *not* be the last? Hope against hope that a new and educated optimism will at last prevail? Or learn (as some have) to live without hope, like Adele, yet enjoy and create and protect what we can?

The more children grow up alert to these questions, and determined to improve on the human performance, the better our chances are. And stories are very important. They take us across the bridge from the thinkable, where we are, to the imaginable, where we need to be.

References

Where given, numbers within parentheses indicate pages in the book cited. Numbers outside the parentheses refer to pages in *The Hidden Teacher*.

Kenneth Allsop, *Silver Flame* (Percival Marshall 1950), 82-4, 85

Kenneth Allsop, *The Sun Himself Must Die* (Latimer House 1950), 84

David Almond, *My Name is Mina* (Hodder 2010), 108

'BB', *Brendon Chase* (Hollis & Carter 1944), 81-2

Nina Bawden, 'The Imprisoned Child', in *The Thorny Paradise* ed. Edward Blishen (Kestrel 1975, pp. 63-4), 34

L.M. Boston, *A Stranger at Green Knowe* (Faber 1961. Page references are to the Puffin edition, 1977), 87-92, 102-3

Julia Briggs, *A Woman of Passion: The Life of E. Nesbit 1858-1924* (Penguin 1989; Hutchinson 1989, p. xi), 55

Dennis Butts, in *The Cambridge Guide to Children's Books in English* (Cambridge University Press 2001, p. 595), 63

Dennis Butts, ed., E. Nesbit, *The Railway Children* (Oxford University Press World's Classics 1991, p. 192), 69

Humphrey Carpenter, *Secret Gardens : A Study of the Golden Age of Children's Literature* (George Allen & Unwin 1985, pp. 137, 16, 133, 135), 55, 57, 59

Children's Literature 18. See page 27.

Richmal Crompton, *William the Bad* (Newnes 1930, Chapter 3), 39-40

Anita Desai, *The Village by the Sea* (Heinemann 1982), 96

Peter Dickinson, *Eva* (Gollancz 1988), 100-103

Bob Dixon, *Catching Them Young 1, Sex, Race and Class in Children's Fiction* (Pluto Press 1977, p. 9), 31-2, 76

G. Bramwell Evens, *A Romany and Raq* (Epworth Press 1930), 79-80

Margery Fisher, *Who's Who in Children's Books* (Weidenfeld & Nicolson 1975), 23

E.M. Forster, 'What I Believe', in *Two Cheers for Democracy* (Edward Arnold 1951 p. 78), 68

Julia Green, *Drawing with Light* (Bloomsbury 2010), 107-8

Graham Greene, *The Lost Childhood and other essays* (Eyre & Spottiswoode 1951), 15

Rob Grunsell, *Born to be Invisible* (Macmillan Education 1978, p. 50), 45

Michael Hayhoe & Stephen Parker, *Reading and Response* (Open University Press, 1990), 14

Peter Hunt, *Children's Literature* (Blackwell 2001, p. 105), 66

Peter Hunt, ed., *Children's Literature: The Development of Criticism*. See page 27.

Fred Inglis, *The Promise of Happiness* (Cambridge University Press 1981, pp. 7, xi, 115), 31, 33, 58-9

Robert Leeson, *Reading and Righting* (Collins 1985, pp. 161, 169-170, 179, 180), 31, 33, 34, 43-5

Aldo Leopold, *A Sand County Almanac* (Oxford University Press [U.S.A.] 1948), 86

C.S. Lewis, 'On Three Ways of Writing for Children', reprinted in *Only Connect* ed. Sheila Egoff et al (Oxford University Press [Canada] 1980, pp. 208, 120), 31, 36

Alison Lurie, *Don't Tell the Grown-Ups: Subversive Children's Literature* (Bloomsbury 1990, pp. 99, 100, 105, 117), 55, 58, 59

Cormac McCarthy, *The Road* (Picador 2006), 106-7

P.W. Musgrave, *From Brown to Bunter: The Life and Death of the School Story* (Routledge & Kegan Paul 1985, p. 17), 39

E. Nesbit, *The Railway Children* (Oxford University Press World's Classics 1991), 52-75

Robert C. O'Brien, *Z for Zachariah* (Gollancz 1975), 100

Susan Price, *From Where I Stand* (Faber 1984, pp. 60, 119), 40, 46-7

Martin Rees, *Our Final Century* (Heinemann 2003, p. 188), 78

Michael Roberts, *The Estate of Man* (Faber 1951, p. 11), 78

Helen Simpson, 'The Boy and the Savage Star' (*Sunday Times*, 22 November 2009), 109

Travellers in Time. See page 27.

Henry Treece, 'Writing for Children', in Owens & Marland (eds.), *The Practice of English Teaching* (Blackie 1970, p. 176), 36-7

Mark Twain, *Huckleberry Finn* (chapter 32), 38-9

Barbara Wall, *The Narrator's Voice. The Dilemma of Children's Fiction* (Macmillan 1991), 24

Gary Waller, *English Poetry of the Sixteenth Century* (Longman 1986, p. 10), 41

Frank Whitehead & others, *Children and Their Books* (Schools Council Report, Macmillan Education 1977), 16

Lightning Source UK Ltd.
Milton Keynes UK
UKOW050020050112

184760UK00001B/56/P